The Poetry of Julia Uceda

Nuestra Voz

Amy Williamsen
General Editor

Vol. 2

PETER LANG
New York • Washington, D.C./Baltimore • San Francisco
Bern • Frankfurt am Main • Berlin • Vienna • Paris

The Poetry of Julia Uceda

Translated, with an Introduction
by Noël Valis

PETER LANG
New York • Washington, D.C./Baltimore • San Francisco
Bern • Frankfurt am Main • Berlin • Vienna • Paris

Library of Congress Cataloging-in-Publication Data

Uceda, Julia.
  [Poems. English & Spanish. Selections]
  The poetry of Julia Uceda/ translated, with an introduction by Noël Valis.
       p. cm.—(Nuestra voz; vol. 2) English and Spanish.
  1. Uceda, Julia—Translations into English. I. Title. II. Series.
PQ6671.C4A28   861'.64—dc20   93-38925
ISBN 0-8204-2409-9
ISSN 1074-6773

Die Deutsche Bibliothek-CIP-Einheitsaufnahme

Uceda, Julia:
[The poetry]
The poetry of Julia Uceda/ transl. and with an introd. by Noël Valis. - New York; Washington, DC/Baltimore; San Francisco; Bern; Frankfurt am Main; Berlin; Vienna; Paris : Lang.
   (Nuestra voz; Vol. 2)
   ISBN 0-8204-2409-9
NE: GT

Cover design by Jorge Sandrini.

The paper in this book meets the guidelines for permanence and durability of the Committee on Production Guidelines for Book Longevity of the Council of Library Resources.

© 1995 Peter Lang Publishing, Inc., New York

All rights reserved.
Reprint or reproduction, even partially, in all forms such as microfilm, xerography, microfiche, microcard, and offset strictly prohibited.

Printed in the United States of America.

Hora

Abrí la puerta
y todo como en mármol
se quedó para siempre.

(Mariposa en cenizas)

Hour

I opened the door
and everything stayed forever,
like it was marble.

(Butterfly in Ashes)

Acknowledgments

Some of these translations first appeared in the following journals:

Prairie Schooner ("Spain is a Long Winter," "Eternal Waves"); *American Poetry Review* ("The Stranger," "Condemned to Silence"); *New Orleans Review* ("The Stranger"); *Ulula* ("Diaspora," "Invitation to the Country of Men"); and *Touchstone* ("The Trap," "Butterfly in Ashes"). "The Stranger" (*APR*) was reprinted in *Anthology of Magazine Verse and Yearbook of American Poetry*, 1986-88 ed.

My thanks go to Octavio Armand for his sensitive reading, to Marianne Grashoff, and above all to Maura Valis Lint for their invaluable help in preparing the manuscript.

The poems in this collection are reprinted here with the kind permission of Julia Uceda.

Table of Contents

Introduction 1

Note on the Translation 12

Selected Bibliography 15

The Poetry of Julia Uceda:

From: *Mariposa en cenizas* ♦ *Butterfly in Ashes*

Ven en el viento ♦ Come Wrapped in the Wind 20

Mis manos, mis labios ♦ My Hands, My Lips 22

El regreso ♦ Return 24

Las hachas ♦ Axes 26

Mariposa en cenizas ♦ Butterfly in Ashes 28

La extraña ♦ The Stranger 30

Los espejos ♦ Mirrors 32

Elegía ♦ Elegy 34

No le pido a los seres perdón por mi existencia. . . ♦
I'm Not Asking Anyone's Pardon For My Existence. . . 36

From: *Extraña juventud* ♦ *Strange Youth*

El acusado ♦ The Accused 38

Extraña juventud ♦ Strange Youth 40

Querido hermano ♦ Dear Brother 42

Diáspora ♦ Diaspora 44

Ved a un hombre ♦ To See a Man 46

En la orilla ♦ On the Border 48

Sé que me roban algo ♦ I Know I'm Being Cheated 52

Respuesta a las brujas ♦ Response for Witches 54

La trampa ♦ The Trap 58

El otro umbral ♦ The Other Threshold 60

From: *Sin mucha esperanza* ♦ *Without Much Hope*

Invitación al país de los hombres ♦
Invitation to the Country of Men 62

La extraña ♦ The Stranger 64

Diálogo ♦ Dialogue 66

Eterno oleaje ♦ Eternal Waves 68

Elegía sobre el tiempo ♦ Elegy Over Time 72

Una patria se ve desde la cumbre ♦
A Country Seen From Afar 78

Cumpleaños ♦ Birthday 86

"No Trespassing" ♦ No Trespassing 90

From: *Poemas de Cherry Lane* ♦ *Cherry Lane Poems*

Noroeste ♦ Northwest 92

Broadway, una noche ♦ Broadway, One Night 96

Rosas del sur ♦ Southern Roses 104

Condenada al silencio ♦ Condemned to Silence 110

Nada se oye ♦ Dead Silence 116

La última cena (Mujer de paja) ♦
The Last Supper (Woman of Straw) 120

Cita con una sombra ♦ Appointment with a Shadow 124

Metamorfosis ♦ Metamorphosis 130

From: *Campanas en Sansueña* ♦ *Bells in Sansueña*

Profundo mar azul ♦ Deep Blue Sea 132

Grupo de hombres (Faculty Meeting) ♦
Group of Men (Faculty Meeting) 144

El tiempo me recuerda ♦ Time Remembers Me 148

España, eres un largo invierno ♦
Spain is a Long Winter 150

Eso ♦ That Thing 154

Si una mariposa se detiene en tu mano, mátala ♦
If a Butterfly Lights on Your Hand, Kill It 156

El rostro vuelto hacia la pared ♦
The Face Turned to the Wall 158

Nota al pie de una historia ♦ Footnote to History . . . 164

Mi positivo es una estrella ♦ My Absolute is a Star . . 168

From: *Viejas voces secretas de la noche* ♦
   Ancient Secret Voices of the Night

Viejas voces secretas de la noche ♦
Ancient Secret Voices of the Night 172

Orden del sueño ♦ The Order of Dream 182

Poemas limítrofes ♦ Limitrophe Poems 184

Los dioses difíciles ♦ The Grounding of Gods 188

Tregua ♦ Truce 196

From: *Del camino de humo* ♦ *Road of Smoke*

Busco señales en la piedra . . . ♦
I Look for Signs in the Stone 198

Profundo como los ríos ♦ Deep Like Rivers 202

Orden del sueño ♦ The Order of Dream 206

CODA

Vitrina ♦ Dollhouse 210

Recuerdo de una calle ♦ Memory of a Street 214

Introduction

*"And a woman walked and walked and walked.
And it was me and not me . . . ."*

—*"Northwest"*

These lines by Julia Uceda are those of a woman alone, a wanderer of uncertain identity who uses connectives like "and" to disconnect and to disperse the inner and outer movement of her sentences. This is a woman who does not know her own name. In an early poem, she remembers "when my name had a place in the air and they called me 'Julia' to give me more room" ("Butterfly in Ashes"). Later she writes in "The Trap": "Julia Uceda, what have you done with your shadow." She is a "woman with no prints," a "body with no name."

Without a name, perhaps — but with an extraordinary passion for being. It seems especially appropriate to begin with this conundrum of identity when speaking of the poetry of Julia Uceda, appropriate first of all in the openly biographical sense. Uceda is not a popularly known poet in her native country of Spain; she lives in seclusion in the northern province of Galicia; and she does not play the intricate game of professional poet that goes with establishing a marketable name in literary circles. Still, like other commentators of her work (García-Posada and Molina Campos, notably), I find it strange that Uceda is not more recognized as an original and intensely visionary poetic voice of contemporary Spain.

Her relative lack of a literary name has deeper reasons and implications, however. Uceda's poetry is dense, especially from the *Cherry Lane Poems* (1968) on. This is difficult and disturbing writing, reflecting a private struggle with the largest question of all, the question of Being. And behind this question, the perplexities of naming and identity. As a passionate, uneaseful meditation on the enigma of existence, such poetry challenges us to go beyond naming, beyond the certainties of categories and schema, for a kind of understanding that partakes of the vivid clarity of dream. Uceda sees her poetry along such visionary lines. She has been compared to José Hierro, with his quasi-surreal technique of the hallucinatory (in *Libro de las alucinaciones*, 1964). But she says,

> for me the dream is an ordering principle of chaos. Reality can be chaotic and a dream can put order into it . . . The difference is that Hierro dreams with his eyes open and I am asleep. I would remove, in my case, the privative 'a' from 'alucinación' [hallucination] and leave it as 'lucinación' [lucination]. Hierro [omits] the temporal plane that corresponds to the present . . . I don't suppress the plane of the real, the quotidian . . . My 'lucinated' poems are often authentic dreams. Dreams I sometimes understand and sometimes not . . . (Molina Campos, "Nocturna luz" 83).

Uceda's *lucinatory* poetry, most tellingly displayed in her last four books—*Cherry Lane Poems* (1968), *Bells in Sansueña* (1977), *Ancient Secret Voices of the Night* (1981), and *Road of Smoke* (1994)—developed slowly out of a long poetic trajectory and within a particular literary and historical context, Franco's Spain. Born in 1925, in the Southern city of Sevilla, Uceda has commented privately in autobiographical notes that she considers herself lucky to have been born in that year. For her

> the decade from 1925 to 1935 was the last to appreciate humanistic and cultural values, individual freedom, science as a form of hope, technology as our salvation and not our destruction . . . They are the last years in Europe that a Visconti or a Bergman could have evoked.

By contrast, her youth and adult years were heavily marked by the repressive Franco regime (1939-75). In an interview, she observed:

> You have to understand what Sevilla was like in those years. [The Franco period] was a very difficult and destructive era, and if we survived . . . it was probably because we were too close to the situation and couldn't compare it to anything else. . . Not only the poets of our generation left Sevilla, the university people too . . ., because they realized how oppressive our situation was. They left for their own good. We were a very unlucky generation . . . .

Uceda spent seven years teaching at Michigan State University (1966-73), eventually settling back in Spain, this time in El Ferrol, where she continues to teach and also heads a small publishing house called Esquío. She has not lived in Sevilla since the mid-sixties.

The other context to mark her was literary, although in truth it would be difficult to separate the literary from the historico-political strands during the Franco era. The contaminating effects of history and ideology burned like acid deep into the writing and art of the period. Uceda has been regarded, chronologically, as part of the Generation of the 1950s, a group of Spanish poets noted especially for their social and political concerns and use of everyday language and imagery. These same poets—writers like Angel González, Manuel Mantero, Gloria Fuertes, and Claudio Rodríguez—also possess a strong existential voice, anticipated in the rehumanizing of poetry expressed in Dámaso Alonso (*Hijos de la ira*, 1944/*Children of Wrath*) and Vicente Aleixandre (*Sombra del paraíso*, 1944/*Shadow of Paradise*), after a brief, post-Civil War neo-classicizing trend.

For Andrew Debicki, the writings of this mid-century generation arise out of the notion of "poetry as an act of discovery and knowledge rather than mere communication" (7). One could argue that communication is almost never "mere" in poetry and can hardly exist without acts of discovery and knowledge. Nevertheless, Debicki's understanding of Spanish poetry of the 50s and 60s is essentially well-founded. Uceda's own poetic trajectory is rooted in this same social and political intentionality, out of which, however, she has gravitated increasingly toward the metaphysical and existential. Critics have also seen her poetry as a working out of questions of knowledge (Molina Campos), as the tracing of a "kind of phenomenology of the spirit" (García-Posada). But what "knowledge," what "acts of discovery"? Here is where Uceda goes her own way, staking out territory in the uncertain, the mysterious, the unnameable. Her experience, especially in the later poetry—whether of knowing or sensing—is a strange kind of non-experience, because the language of poetry does not allow her entry into zones of being that cannot constitute "acts" of discovery and knowledge. They simply are.

Something must be said, also, of Uceda's position as a woman writing in Spain. Both Carmen Conde and Ana María Fagundo, poets of distinction themselves, point to the lack of group identity, the feeling of isolation in which many Spanish women poets seem to have worked during the Franco period in particular. Conde suggests—in 1970—that the absence of solidarity or of a consciously formed generation of women writers is not important. "To be of one's time" is, however (Conde 232). But "to be of one's time" in 1970 was a major tenet of many poets then; indeed, it was a largely generational preoccupation. Uceda's second collection of poetry is dedicated to "[e]l hombre de mi tiempo," "To people everywhere now" (Strange Youth, 1962). "To be of one's time" implies belonging, willingly or not, to the social fabric that makes and breaks us—and that we in turn make and break. Women writers in Spain were no different in this sense than their male counterparts. All were generational in that context. But what is harder to detect is a sense of awareness, of conscious cohesiveness among women poets of the Franco period. This circumstance may very well be changing now, with the existence of women's publishing houses like Torremozas and laSal, the increasingly influential Instituto de la Mujer (Women's Institute), and cooperative bookstores run by women, such as the Librería Mujeres in Madrid or the Llibreria de Dones in Barcelona.

What institutionalization can do to foment a sense of solidarity today, friendship did more than a century and a half ago in Spain. For a brief time, at the height of the romantic age, poets like Carolina Coronado, Gertrudis Gómez de Avellaneda, Robustiana Armiño, and Vicenta García Miranda, created among themselves such solidarity through letter writing, articles, the circulation of their poetry and dedication of poems to one another (see Susan Kirkpatrick's fine study). This informal network of poetic sisterhood is reflected thematically in many poems, and contrasts startlingly with the solitariness of women writers in Uceda's time. Woman as the standard-bearer of tradition and the family was of course the prevailing dogma of both the nineteenth century and the Franco era. But romanticism and a short-lived yet intense wave of liberalism encouraged women of the 1830s and 40s to write for the first time both as individuals and as members of a group. Over a century later, women writers were still frowned upon and considered unnatural, yet they persisted during the long silence of Franco's winter. Uceda's image of herself as "la extraña"—in the dual sense of "strange" and "stranger"—is not only existentialist in nature. It is also deeply grounded in the cultural circumstances of her time in which she, as a nonconforming Spaniard *and* as a woman writing, lived.

Another way to distinguish further between the felt cohesiveness of the women romantics and the fragmented singularity of their post-Civil War successors (taken in an ample sense) is to see how each poetic constituency grapples with its understanding of experience. Despite numerous restrictions of a socio-political and literary nature, women poets of the early nineteenth century felt great excitement over the possibilities of sudden historic aperture. We know of course that stifling conventions of gender soon overwhelmed all but a few of them, most notably Gertrudis Gómez de Avellaneda, Carolina Coronado and, later, Rosalía de Castro; but even a strict gender code of writing, as Susan Kirkpatrick has pointed out, could be subverted and made over into an intense expression of romantic subjectivity. Poetic experience was in this way a function of poetic en-gendering.

But the triumph of Franco meant for many a devastating historic closure. For many life stopped and a forty-year wall of isolation grew around the country. This particular set of historical events, lodged like a flint in the heart of Spain, sparked immediate and enduring opposition. Opposition naturally took many forms, but one way to resist was simply to show how time seemed to stop. Deceptively passive as a critique of the regime, the suggestion of stasis in Spanish society, nonetheless, held deeper implications when it surfaced in imaginative literature. The chiselled and still perfections of neo-classic verse produced in the immediate post-Civil War years are often judged now as escapist literature. But where did that evasive sense of verbal stasis come from? Two decades later, novelist Luis Martín-Santos continued to play off such stasis in *A Time of Silence* (1961) by converting a cancerous society into a metaphor of metastasis. The mutations of cells provided readers with a biological-physical space of the imagination—imagination turned into a medium growing awareness, the seeds of consciousness. This double-vision of cells—the tissue of life—transformed into a pathology of death, the cell of imprisonment, is a remarkable example of the effects of forced historical stasis. (In an entirely different context one is reminded of Sharon Olds' vivid use of similar imagery in *The Gold Cell*, 1987.)

Reading Julia Uceda's poetry, one has the sense of history taking away the possibilities of experience. The result is the terrible bereftment of the unlived life. This motif of the "unlived life" is one that critic Edward Engelberg identifies as paramount from the romantics on. As "elegiac fictions," such writings regardless of genre express the particular "modern sense of personal loss and dispossession, and . . . a special kind of sadness that validates the belief that one's life has been a series of missed opportunities" (*Elegiac Fictions* 2). This "elegizing of the self" Freud called "melancholia," observing that "in mourning it is the world which has become poor and empty; in melancholia it is the ego itself" (246). Engelberg's provocative study centers on the endless variations of narcissism as it manifests itself in the paradoxical yet no less mournful loss of loss itself, of life unlived. The modern sadness of the wasted life is often accompanied for complex reasons by the idea of history itself as a waste, by a consciousness of history's burden as Nietzsche would have it (Engelberg 14-16).

Engelberg's narcissistic characterization of the unlived life, however, does not hold in cases like Julia Uceda's, where the burden of history is truly a *thing* that weighs heavily, oppressively, over men and women. History as oppression, in all its forms of dictatorship, tyranny, totalitarian action, doesn't enter into Engelberg's scheme of the "unlived life." The complexities of narcissism alone in literature cannot explain the unlived life as it is understood under stifling regimes like Franco's. Thus in "Strange Youth" ("Extraña juventud"), Uceda begins: "Plunge your hands into the water/of time. Get to the very bottom/of the future passing." And she ends with "lips on which pain stops,/that tell you something strange/is not happening here."

This acute consciousness of stasis is sometimes translated as silence in her work. In "Dear Brother" ("Querido hermano") she writes an imaginary letter to an absent brother whose implied dissidence is heard when "our parents talk loudly to erase the site/of your silence." "An air of silence veils our speech," she says, "though we all have permission to yell,/to pass through the idea you don't exist." In another poem, the sense of privation is felt as personal theft—"I Know I'm Being Cheated" ("Sé que me roban algo"): "Of this earth I'm being cheated,/of these fields that smell like/deserted death." And later she says: "I know that somewhere,/someone wants me weak/to tame my blood./To cheat me of this life . . . ." In one of her most powerful poems, "Condemned to Silence" ("Condenada al silencio"), she ends on this tense note of contraries: "What's strange is this:/when you can't collapse on the sidewalk/because order must be maintained in public." Is life sudden collapse, and history as practised by petty *generalissimos* the order of paralysis? And finally, in a scatological, haunting vision of Spain as a "long winter," she writes explicitly about her country: "'Look, man,/if you come to this country, go back, abort,/so they don't fish you out of the void and bring you/to this place, dragged by the ears./In this eternal snow/flowers die and gods laugh.'/Never Spain—her sleep—/only a fat devouring worm."

Here is the unlived life when history in all its unbearable particulars does not permit you to live. Like Martín-Santos, Uceda beautifully exploits the traditional Iberian preoccupation with death by linking it to a specific historical reenactment of life as death. This temporalizing of death politicizes her poetry—a point which earlier commentators have discreetly avoided for the most part—allowing us as well to see her work as part of a larger, twentieth-century lament for all such collective and individual deaths perpetrated in killing fields, gas ovens, and lonely beaches.

But Uceda is also a survivor of this unlived life. Drawing on Heideggerian insights, she deepens the circumstances of stagnating history by rooting it within the modern estrangement from Being. Her poetry turns on the paradox of writing from and into that which is not experienced. Poetry that dwells on the passion of being and the elegy of time as does Uceda's work is usually called metaphysical. It has a long tradition, starting with the English metaphysical poets Crashaw, Herbert, Marvell and

Donne and some of the Golden Age Spanish poets, passing to Hopkins, Unamuno and Machado, and, more recently, Luis Cernuda. The poetry of meditation has moved from contemplation of the divine presence to an increasingly more radicalized secularization of the poetic gift. What has not changed is the grounding of poetic meditation in places or settings arising out of the chambers of memory.

These memory rooms, once used as mnemonic techniques for mastering oratory and other forms of discourse, are mental reconstructions of the scene between self and God, or in twentieth-century poetry, between self and self. In Uceda's poetry, "place" is another way of getting at Being by recognizing that we never do get at Being. For "place" in Uceda is dis-placement, wandering, bumping against doors, windows, walls, and never arriving—a reflection, too, of the twentieth-century's historic mass movements of homelessness and exile. It is remarkable how the places of meditative poetry coincide with the existential tropes of Heidegger's thinking about Being. "'Being there,'" he writes, "names that which should first of all be experienced, and subsequently thought of, as a place—namely, the location of the truth of Being" (213). For the author of *Being and Time*, this expressively felt concreteness is offset, however, by the horror of modern oblivion of Being.

Uceda's knowledge of Heidegger is clear. One of the two epigraphs for *Strange Youth* comes from Heidegger: "We have arrived too late for the gods and too soon for Being. Man is a poem begun by Being." This feeling of incompleteness, of distance from Being, permeates the poetry of Uceda. As in Heidegger, she makes no attempt to define Being, a futile exercise in any case. She can only talk about revelation out of darkness, the night possessing its own light, its own knowledge, or as she puts it, "night is a walking/looking for angles of light." This nocturnal light is akin to Heidegger's "light of Being." We never "get" to the light, just as Uceda's poetic persona never ceases moving without arriving, but "the light itself is considered sufficiently illuminated as soon as we recognize that we look through it whenever we look at beings" (Heidegger 207).

The closest we come to Being is through the presentness of beings, through temporality. *Dasein* is "being there," being "thrown into" existence with no particular reason why. "And all this lying about on the beach,/just to die one day," writes Uceda. "They say that maybe over there.../But I say, I'm alive now./It's here, on this earth, where I am,/where I know myself,/where I'm dying/a little more every second" ("I Know I'm Being Cheated"/"Sé que me roban algo"). Uceda's answer to this "thrownness into Being" is not an answer; it's more like a stance. Seeing the void—"Why is there any being at all and not rather Nothing?," Heidegger asks (219)—she writes: "The void is not a chair/facing the desert: it is the silence/of the soul. It is a heart/without light" ("Limitrophe Poems"/"Poemas limítrofes"). Without light—then, without Being. But elsewhere she speaks of our pain, unavoidable, how we cry "because we haven't learned to be dragged in silence/by water that doesn't flow from life/or lead to life or to its name, because we weep/for what neither leaf nor bird,/nor wounded deer nor soundless fish weeps" ("The Face Turned to the Wall"/"El rostro vuelto hacia la pared"). This pain marks our authenticity existentially speaking. Then how do we endure?

There are beings, Heidegger writes,

> who stand open for the openness of Being in which they stand, by standing it. This 'standing it,' this enduring, is experienced under the name of 'care.' The ecstatic essence of being there is approached by way of care...(214).

Here is the passion of Being according to Uceda, in "Footnote to History" ("Nota al pie de una historia"): "The last goodbye has/begun. They're going to say/the formulas of the finish. And I will have/to leave it all when I hear: 'Consumatum/est.' I understand now,/finally, the joy/of being among you, harsh shadows,/beings who pass by me/in cities, at night./Trees, rocks, roses, I understand the joy/of your being next to me with your elusive/presence that, as a child,/I could not understand when I played/with you...." And later: "I bathe in space, light, crystal/air, long/silences, passing/rivers:/all the beauty that is mine now, to live."

This Heideggerian endurance, in which we, like the poet, find ourselves, is a way of *not* finding ourselves at the same time. We are placed in this situation—"thrown into" it—only to find dis-placement, diaspora. "Who can guarantee that I am not just a name," Uceda writes in the appropriately named "Diaspora," "who can find me, for certain, in the battered ribs/of my shadow." "A bored hand left me on the ground/ . . . chained to a thirst for forbidden words,/words waiting for a signal . . . ." Naming identifies, but Uceda is looking for something that goes beyond naming, that is nameless. This namelessness is Being itself.

In one poem she calls it "That Thing" ("Eso"): "That thing they screamed at a long time ago: get out!/That, that thing there, on the border,/why does it persist, still,/in moving up/from the darkness to the light that doesn't belong to it?" A few lines later, she writes: "What is that thing,/what's it made of,/that it still floats, climbs,/breathes and nearly/smiles and leans/into the color of the poppy?" In "The Faced Turned to the Wall," she says that "It has no name./It's you and me. It will be and was everyone." "It's water and it isn't water." And then: "It was here from the beginning./And it's like thirst."

Uceda goes to the limits of language, she writes "Limitrophe Poems," she bangs against the edges of her body seeing her body overrun by a "black door." Thus in "Ancient Secret Voices of the Night," she says: ". . . I don't understand/why this door is growing inside my body./(A door that is much larger than my body./A door that overflows my shape.)/I don't knock at this door, or scratch it, or shout./I wait." And she ends with these lines: "A door in the form of a shadow./A question in the form of a door./A question darkened with distance." Body plays against non-body here just as death plays against life in other poems. Yet dualities dissolve in Uceda's work. " . . . [N]o one knows what/life is called among the dead," she writes in "No Trespassing." When she goes to meet a friend in "Appointment with a Shadow" ("Cita con una sombra"), a voice tells her she *"will pass a cemetery/and on the right* . . . ." She crosses "an uncountable sleeping census," keeps looking for her friend's door, which seems "to recede, very slowly, from [her] raised/fist

. . . ." The poem ends: "My friend,/between you and my visit,/so many deaths." This intermingling of life and death, corporality and non-corporality, represents neither denial nor affirmation of one or the other. How can one assume either if we lack the names for both of them? Nevertheless, this unnamed experience does not lessen "the pain of matter disintegrating" ("Deep Blue Sea"/"Profundo mar azul").

In some ways, like another writer of her time, Brazilian novelist Clarice Lispector, Uceda is attempting to describe "an experience without knowing what it [is], an experience that might better be described as a non-experience" (Paulson 521). In an elegant essay on "Closing the Circle: Science, Literature, and the Passion of Matter," Paulson writes that

> Lispector calls on language to evoke that which is so simple and fundamental that it has no name. Her novel is an approach to the unnameable thingness of those things that bear ordinary names, an attempt to work back from words toward that part of experience always left behind by even the simplest acts of naming, intending, and giving meaning (520).

While Paulson refers to Lispector's *The Passion According to G.H.* (*A paixão segundo G.H.*, 1964), he could easily be talking about Julia Uceda's poetry.

The "passion of matter" in Lispector becomes the "passion of being" in Uceda, as matter and being fuse into the "twinned tree," with two trunks, that the poet calls herself in "Ancient Secret Voices of the Night." For Heidegger the "truth of Being" is the "ground in which metaphysics, as the root of the tree of philosophy, is kept and from which it is nourished" (208). Uceda takes that tree—that "location of the truth of Being"—and makes it the place of her poetry. It is a place unquestionably tied to historical and literary realities yet cognizant that there is "another place": "What ties/my attention to another place/isn't what I'd call memory./It's more like a root:/the root of a chained memory,/. . ./a root that I should never question/simply jump over/because the weave of its veins poses deep enigmas,/and time is grasping my wrist/as testimony/of brief but certain obligation" ("Limitrophe Poems"). This intense engagement with the temporal, with the matter of our residence on earth, is Uceda's own "way back" into the ground of her Being.

A Note on the Translation

This selection is intended as a representative sampling of Uceda's poetry from her first book, *Mariposa en cenizas*, published in 1959, to her latest work, *Del camino de humo* (1994). I have translated in its entirety *Viejas voces secretas de la noche* (1981) to keep the sense of interconnectedness between the individual poems of the volume. In one case—"Una patria se ve desde la cumbre," from *Sin mucha esperanza*—I used the slightly modified version indicated by Uceda's handwritten revisions in the copy she gave me. As a coda, two poems, previously unpublished ("Recuerdo de una calle" and "Vitrina"), are also included.

I have tried, throughout, to keep the strangeness of her poetry in the (sometimes) strangeness of my translation. Uceda's carefully chosen imagery is often mysterious, arising as it does out of the "order of dream." In a single poem the registers of tone and diction can vary significantly, producing quiet disruptions from line to line. The mixing of everyday language with a more abstract, philosophical vocabulary reinforces the sense of the complex and the difficult beneath the apparent simplicity of plain speech. Unadorned syntax rubs against intense, strange metaphors. Lines in the form of questions remain unanswered. An unusual usage of enjambement and dashes intentionally breaks up the expected smooth reading, the connections between words (see Peñas-Bermejo 66-67). How to retain this strangeness without making Uceda's poetry incomprehensible or stiff and awkward, continually challenged my translating efforts.

I decided, finally, to steer a middle course, opting for overall "readability" while suggesting through imagery, selective enjambement, a pared-down, sometimes stark syntax, and other devices, the rare intensity of Uceda's poetic vision. Like William Weaver in his translating approach to Carlo Emilio Gadda, I have tried *not* "to clarify the meaning when [the poet] has deliberately made it murky..." (119).

Take, for example, the second stanza of the poem, "Dead Silence" ("Nada se oye"): "¿Fui—fuimos—entre la niebla/que fingía triunfantes/contornos a mi lado: un rostro puro,/muy extraño en su noche, con los signos/de un idioma remoto en su frente, en su boca?" The translator is immediately confronted with an interrupted flow signaled by the use of the dash in the first line. Next the fog or mist image ("niebla") takes on an oddly active role as the subject of the verb "fingía." The imagery that follows is simple enough to read at first, but hard to understand afterward. What is a "rostro puro/muy extraño en su noche, con los signos/de un idioma remoto en su frente, en su boca," which translated word for word is: "a pure face,/very strange in its night, with the signs/of a remote language on its forehead, on its mouth"? To bring out more forcefully Uceda's deliberate disturbance of an unreflective reading, I came up with: "a pure-face,/night strange, with signs/of a remote language on its forehead and mouth." In rendering the original as a hyphenated "pure-face," modified by "night strange," I hoped to suggest the feeling of mysterious offcenteredness in Uceda's poem, while retaining legibility in the rest of the stanza. Likewise, I left the interruptive dash in line one, but removed the notion of agency from the fog image—which sounded awkward in English—and instead used a descriptive modifier ("a fog of pretend profiles"). (In the process I dropped the original enjambement of "triunfantes/ contornos" as too heavy-handed in English.)

I also had to decide whether to use rhyme for the few poems written mostly in assonance. These appear in Uceda's early work, after which free verse predominates. English rhyming schemes would, I felt, have conventionalized the visionary oddness of these poems. Moreover, assonance is so uniquely Spanish that it seemed a more discreet gesture to recognize its untranslatable qualities. There is one exception: the poem, "Vitrina," loosely rendered as "Dollhouse" since "display cabinet" or "showcase" did not speak to the poem's delicate evocation of a fragile and strangely unreal lost past. With rhyme I wanted to call attention not only to the existence of assonance (a-a) throughout, but to the nostalgic, gently ironic view of loss incorporated into the poem.

Gregory Rabassa has remarked that "translation is a disturbing craft because there is precious little certainty about what we are doing . . . " (12). A translation, he says, "is never finished . . . " (7). This sense of the tentative, of process, argues against closure, against the definitive reading and readability of translated texts, and I hope, parallels and reflects the same open-endedness which, in turn, marks Julia Uceda's poetry.

Selected Bibliography

Julia Uceda:

Poetry:

Mariposa en cenizas. Prologue by Manuel Mantero. Arcos de la Frontera: Alcaraván, 1959.

Extraña juventud. Madrid: Rialp, 1962.

Sin mucha esperanza. Madrid: Agora, 1966.

Poemas de Cherry Lane. Madrid: Agora, 1968.

Campanas en Sansueña. Madrid: Dulcinea, 1977.

Viejas voces secretas de la noche. El Ferrol: Esquío, 1981.

Julia Uceda: Poesía. Ed. Francisco J. Peñas-Bermejo. El Ferrol: Esquío, 1991.

Del camino de humo. Sevilla: Renacimiento, 1994.

Criticism:

Antología poética de José Luis Hidalgo. Edition, with Introduction, by Julia Uceda. Madrid: Aguilar, 1970.

"Aproximaciones a la poesía de Jorge Guillén," in *La expresión.* By Jorge Guillén. El Ferrol: Esquío, 1981.

Criticism on Julia Uceda:

Cano, José Luis. "La poesía de Julia Uceda." *Insula* No. 378 (May 1978): 8-9.

García Montero, Luis. "Uceda, Julia." *Diccionario de literatura española e hispanoamericana*. 2. Ed. Ricardo Gullón. Madrid: Alianza, 1993. 1643.

García-Posada, Miguel. "*Viejas voces secretas de la noche.*" *ABC* (10 Sept. 1983): IV.

Josia, Vincenzo. "Julia Uceda Valiente." *Poeti sivigliani di oggi*. Roma: Opere Nuove, 1966. 145-47.

Mantero, Manuel. "Julia Uceda y lo extraño." *Poesía española contemporánea. Estudio y antología (1939-1965)*. Barcelona: Plaza y Janés, 1966. 179-82.

_____ "Transmigración y sueños en la poesía de Julia Uceda." *Salina* No. 7 (Dec. 1993): 63-66.

Miró, Emilio. "Crónica de poesía." *Insula* No. 264 (Nov. 1968): 6.

Molina Campos, Enrique. "Dos grandes poetisas andaluzas: Elena y Julia." *Cal* No. 25 (Jan. 1978): 24-27.

_____ "Nocturna luz de la poesía de Julia Uceda." *Nueva Estafeta* No. 41 (April 1982): 80-84.

Pérez, Janet. "Uceda, Julia." *Dictionary of the Literature of the Iberian Peninsula*. 2. Ed. Germán Bleiberg, Maureen Ihrie, and Janet Pérez. Westport, CT: Greenwood Press, 1993. 1627-28.

Ruiz-Copete, Juan de Dios. "Julia Uceda, o la poesía de la existencia." *Poetas de Sevilla*. Sevilla: Servicio de Publicaciones de la Caja de Ahorros Provincial San Fernando de Sevilla, 1971. 251-62.

Valis, Noël. "Uceda, Julia." *Women Writers of Spain*. Ed. Carolyn L. Galerstein. New York: Greenwood Press, 1986. 319-20.

_____ "Julia Uceda." *An Encyclopedia of Continental Women Writers*. 2. Ed. Katharina M. Wilson. New York: Garland, 1991. 1257-58.

Other References:

Conde, Carmen. "Poesía femenina española, viviente." *Arbor* No. 294 (June 1970): 221-32.

Debicki, Andrew P. *Poetry of Discovery. The Spanish Generation of 1956-71*. Lexington: University Press of Kentucky, 1982.

Engelberg, Edward. *Elegiac Fictions. The Motif of the Unlived Life*. University Park: Pennsylvania State University Press, 1989.

Fagundo, Ana María. "Poesía femenina española siglo XX." *Alaluz* No. 5 (Spring-Fall 1987-88): 5-13.

Freud, Sigmund. "Mourning and Melancholia." *Standard Edition of the Complete Psychological Works*. Trans. James Strachey. v. 14. London: The Hogarth Press, 1957.

Heidegger, Martin. "The Way Back Into the Ground of Metaphysics." *Existentialism from Dostoevsky to Sartre*. Ed. and Trans. Walter Kaufmann. 1956; New York: World Publishing Co., 1966.

Kirkpatrick, Susan. *Las Románticas. Women Writers and Subjectivity in Spain, 1835-1850*. Berkeley: University of California Press, 1989.

Paulson, William. "Closing the Circle: Science, Literature, and the Passion of Matter." *New England Review and Bread Loaf Quarterly* 12 (Summer 1990): 512-26.

Rabassa, Gregory. "No Two Snowflakes Are Alike: Translation as Metaphor." *The Craft of Translation*. Ed. John Biguenet and Rainer Schulte. Chicago: University of Chicago Press, 1989. 1-12.

Weaver, William. "The Process of Translation." *The Craft of Translation*. 117-24.

The Poetry of Julia Uceda

From: *Mariposa en cenizas*

Ven en el viento

En el lagar pequeño de mi mano
zumo de esquilas y naranjos tengo.
La vida se derrama por mis brazos.
Ven en el viento.

En el ala sombría de mi nuca
rumor de algas y de voces dejo.
Te abrirán los caminos de mi alma.
Ven en el viento.

Largos suspiros pasan. Me sacuden.
Ya mis hojas son pájaros huyendo.
El tiempo va de huída y pisa y tala.
Ven en el viento.

From: *Butterfly in Ashes*

Come Wrapped in the Wind

My hand is the palm of a wine press,
holding the juices of prawns and oranges.
Life is spilling down my arms.
Come wrapped in the wind.

The nape of my neck is a shaded wing,
leaving a rustle of weeds and voices,
to open the paths of my soul to you.
Come wrapped in the wind.

Long sighs pass, shaking me.
My leaves are birds fleeing.
Time slips away, stamps down and strips bare.
Come wrapped in the wind.

Mis manos, mis labios

Podaré mis manos
con tu silencio.

Sellaré mis labios
con tu silencio.

Quemaré mi cuerpo
con tu silencio.

Volverás un día
de agosto o enero.

Buscando los vivos
hallarás los muertos.

Seguirá tus pasos
un largo silencio.

Tu largo, tu enorme
terrible silencio.

My Hands, My Lips

I will clip my hands
with your silence.

I will seal my lips
with your silence.

I will burn my body
with your silence.

You will return one day
in August or January.

Seeking the living
you will find the dead.

In your footsteps there follows
a long silence.

Your long and terrible
Siberian silence.

El regreso

A Manuel Mantero

¿Verdad que yo debiera morir
ahora que el tiempo es como un ascua pura,
ahora que el cielo es un gesto total de bienvenida?
Sin embargo, yo pienso en la noche,
en los vagos caminos de la noche
por los que iré perdiéndome, borrándome.
Y quedará a mi espalda . . . nada.
Un silencio. Un vacío. Un mundo no creado.

¿O no? ¿Podré tal vez un día
correr, como una niebla silenciosa,
desde el mar a la tierra,
abrazando los altos pinos
que hoy no me ven ni me conocen?

Secretamente, creo que volveré.
Con mis cabellos duros
jugarán las estrellas y las fuentes
y yo seré un misterio más en los misterios,
hoja en hoja, sonido en aire, tierra . . .

Y tal vez dentro de un hogar,
el hombre joven diga a la mujer:
Cierra ya la ventana. Esta es noche
de nieblas y de brujas. Ven.
Y ámame.

Return

For Manuel Mantero

Must I really die
now that time is like a pure burning coal,
now that the sky
is a wide palm of welcome?
And then I think of night,
the blurred byways of night
where I'll go and lose myself in blankness.
And at my back . . . nothing.
Silence. Void. World not there.

Maybe not? Maybe I'll drift
one day, like silent mist,
from the sea to the land,
clinging to tall pines
that do not see me,
do not know me?

Secretly, I believe that I'll return.
Fountains and stars will play
with my stiff hair
and I'll be one more mystery among mysteries,
leaf among leaves, sound in air, earth . . .

And maybe in a house somewhere,
a young man says to his wife:
Shut that window. This is a night
for mists and witches. Come,
and love me.

Las hachas

Esta tristeza de mi cuerpo (dónde estás, muerte mía),
esta tristeza de mi cuerpo, de este árbol que soy,
la fue mordiendo, en los largos inviernos del corazón,
el hacha negra del silencio,
el hacha roja de la desesperación,
el hacha gris de los sueños
que se fueron como barcos de lluvia. Y no volvieron.

Esta alegría de mis ojos (dónde estás, amor mío),
que hace vibrar las hojas de este árbol que soy,
surgió en las breves y extrañas primaveras del mundo,
cuando me mirabas con tus ojos,
cuando me tocabas con tu voz,
cuando me alzabas con tu beso.
Y así he vivido y muerto tantas veces
como venías o te ibas.

Yo te amaré también—en árbol o en pájaro—
cuando mi pie descanse en otras islas
—en las islas en que el agua es una eternidad
sin muertos;
paraísos de espumas sin ahogados—
y allí te cantaré—con mi voz o con la del viento—
y me conocerás—y nos conoceremos—
sin recordar mi nombre,
como a algo perdido en otra vida
que tampoco recuerdas.

Axes

This sadness of my body (where have you gone, death
[of mine),
this sadness of my body, this tree that is me,
this was splintered, in the heart's long winters,
by the black axe of silence,
the red axe of despair,
the gray axe of dreams
that sailed away like rain-boats. And didn't return.

This joy in my eyes (where have you gone, love of mine),
that makes the leaves of the tree that is me quiver,
was born in the world's brief, strange springs,
when you looked at me with your eyes,
when you touched me with your voice,
when you lifted me with your kiss.
I've lived and died so many times
in the wake of your presence.

I'll love you still—as a tree or a bird—
when my feet come to rest on other islands
—islands where water is eternity
without the dead;
foamy shoals of paradise without the drowned—
and there I'll sing to you—with my voice or with the wind—
and you'll know me—we'll know each other—
without my name,
like something lost in another life
you've also forgotten.

Mariposa en cenizas

Hoy te escribo, Señor, y te pregunto
por la escondida luna de mi muerte;
por sus manos de hielos afilados
como agujas que cosen telarañas;
por esa muerte mía, sólo mía,
que aún no está madura por tus campos.

Tú, Dios, para matarme,
para volverme a Ti y a la sombría
cuna de donde vine, has de abrasar mis alas
y desatarme en nube pálida de ceniza
y aplastarme en la luz última de una tarde.

Y yo he de bailar,
con mi vestido gris de polvo y niebla,
frente al cielo amarillo y el sol frío,
sobre tus rosas y arrayanes muertos,
arrastrando mis alas desgarradas
igual que un breve cisne de las flores.

Y te pondré en la mano
dos lágrimas de luz y sal, como un pequeño
quejido por mis alas ardidas ya y cenizas
desde que me las diste un octubre lejano.

Cuando tuvo mi nombre un lugar en el aire
y me llamaron "Julia" para hacerme más sitio.

Butterfly in Ashes*

I write today to you, Lord, and I ask
about the masked moon of my death;
about hands of ice filed sharp
like needles for sewing webs;
about that death of mine, mine alone,
which still isn't ripe in your fields.

God, for you to kill me,
and send me back to You, to the shadow cradle
I came from, you've got to set my wings on fire
and free me in pale clouds of ash,
then crush me in the last light of day.

And I'll be dancing,
in my gray dress of dust and mist,
face to the yellow sky and the cold sun,
over your dead roses and white myrtle,
dragging my torn wings
like a fugitive swan in flower.

And in your hand I'll set
two tears of light and salt, like a small
plaint for my wings, so seared, and ashes
when you gave them to me one distant October.

When my name had a place in the air
and they called me "Julia" to give me more room.

---

*An allusion to Góngora's "Butterfly in ashes freed" ("Mariposa en cenizas desatada"), *Soledades* (*Solitudes*).

La extraña

Siempre fui una extraña.
A veces me creía de la mano de todos,
entre luces y sombras,
mi voz entre las voces.
Una amistad de corazón de pájaro
empapaba mis manos.

Y de pronto las cosas me volvieron la espalda,
dejándome en el centro de una luz
tan pálida, tan fría. . .
Como de huesos.
Como de peces recién muertos.
Temblaba allí. Miraba
el detrás de las cosas,
las nucas, las espaldas,
los talones extraños,
el confuso revés de las sonrisas,
el secreto más triste y polvoriento
que nadie se confiesa. No podía
salir de aquella luz en la que nada
parecía—ni era—como antes.

¿Por qué yo?
Se me helaban
los labios de tristeza.
¡Si existiera
sin mirarme existir! . . .
Tal vez para tan poco . . .

Cuando de nuevo la luz se hacía
y mi cuerpo giraba de la mano de todos
—entre luces y sombras,
mi voz entre las voces—
un lejano recuerdo me oprimía.
Sigo siendo una extraña.

The Stranger

I was always a stranger.
I used to think I was held in everyone's hands,
among lights and shadows,
my voice mixed with voices.
Like a bird's heart
friendship soaked my hands.

And suddenly things turned their back on me.
I was alone in the center of a light
so pale, so cold . . .
Like it was bones.
Like it was fish just died.
I trembled. I stared
at the backs of things,
napes, spines,
odd heels
the blurred wrong side out of smiles,
secrets so sad and dirty
no one can confess them. Escape
from that light in which nothing
seemed—nor was—as before, was impossible.

Why me?
My lips froze shut
with grief.
What if I existed
and couldn't see myself exist!
Maybe, for something so small . . .

When the light came on again
and my body turned in everyone's hands
—among lights and shadows,
my voice mixed with voices—
a memory, far off, still weighed me down.
I am always a stranger.

Los espejos

Pude no haber nacido.
¿Quién me robó del sueño?
Me sacaron un día
de otoño del misterio.
Breves llamas de oro
llovían sobre el suelo.
Sujeta a este horizonte
infinito de espejos.
Siempre palpan mis manos
las paredes de hielo.

Mirrors

I might not have been born.
Who stole me away from the dream?
One day in fall
they dragged me out of the mystery.
Quick flames of gold
rained over the ground.
I am chained to this infinite
horizon of mirrors.
My hands keep tapping
the ice on the walls.

Elegía

Tengo huesos de luz entre las manos,
calavera de un sueño. Calavera
de toda una sumisa primavera
desplomada en heleros. Niños canos,

menhires de la pena, lirios vanos
que disteis en la nada y en su era,
amados sueños, adorada cera,
también yo estoy difunta entre mis manos.

Un mar de huesos, de recuerdos, se alza
en mármoles heridos por auroras
que huyen de la muerte y de su aliento.

La muerte llegará, ciega y descalza,
no oiremos sus pisadas destructoras . . .
Nuestro sepulcro quedará en el viento.

Elegy

I hold bones of light in my hands,
the skull of a dream. The skull
of one submissive spring
sunk into snowcaps. Graying children,

menhirs of pain, vain lilies
that fell in the void, in the garden,
beloved dreams, like sweet wax,
I too am dead in my hands.

A sea of bones, of memories, rises
in marble wounded by daybreak
in flight from death and breath.

Death will come, blind and barefoot,
we won't hear its devouring footsteps . . .
Our grave is buried in the wind.

*No le pido a los seres perdón
por mi existencia . . .*

No le pido a los seres perdón por mi existencia.
La levanto y la empuño como a un viento domado.
Antes que ser un árbol, antes que inexistencia,
este calor de establo de mi pecho pisado.

Existir sobre todo. Adoro la presencia
de la luz que la sombra quisiera haber cegado,
el rumor de mi sangre, la dulce incontinencia
del labio que otra carne quisiera sepultado.

Yo no pido disculpas por mi ser sin medida,
por mi ser oceánico, por mis ansias de vida,
por la vida caliente que se quema en las horas.

Y seguiré viviendo aunque madres horrendas
clamen sobre los montes, rasguen rostros y vendas
y suelten sobre el mundo tijeras destructoras.

I'm Not Asking Anyone's Pardon For My Existence...

I'm not asking anyone's pardon for my existence.
I alone raise and grasp it like I'm taming the wind.
Before a tree is, before existence is,
there is this warmth of the stable squeezed into my breast.

Above all, to exist. I love the presence
of light that shadow would blind,
the rush of my blood, the sweet flow
of lips that other flesh would bury.

I'm not begging excuses for my self unbounded,
for my oceans of being, for my craving of life,
for the heat of life that burns hours and hours.

And I will keep on living even if vile mothers
cry out from the hills, claw at their faces and veils
and let loose upon the world the slashing of scissors.

From: *Extraña juventud*

El acusado

Está en el centro de la luz. Frío quirófano,
la tierra huye bajo él, que cae sin destino
mientras cien focos buscan sus más puros secretos
y los puños se alzan contra su sien de arena.
Manos, índices, puños, golpes, pasos, palabras
—dónde una rosa para asir la vida—.
Manos, círculos, voces, ruedas, botas, aceros.
Y ni el llanto de un niño. Ni una lágrima a punto.
Indices como agujas le señalan el cuerpo:
de qué tiene la culpa. Le señalan los ojos:
qué mirada es culpable. Le señalan la frente:
creó un Dios. Le señalan lo más limpio del pecho,
abren todos sus sueños y señalan al fondo.
Le señalan los dientes, le señalan la lengua,
con ira le señalan los asaltados miembros,
arrancan mariposas del terror de su vientre,
escupen en la histórica contextura del labio
y le indican su sitio: una soga pendiente.
Oye una voz unánime: "es Dios quien te lo manda".
Y ni el llanto de un niño. Ni una lágrima a punto.

From: *Strange Youth*

The Accused

He's in the center of the light. A cold operating room,
the earth flees beneath him, drifting he falls
while a hundred spotlights probe his purest secrets
and fists are raised against his temples of sand.
Hands, fingers, fists, blows, steps, words,
—where's the rose to seize life—.
Hands, circles, voices, wheels, boots, steel.
And not even a child's crying. Or a single tear.
Fingers like needles stab his body:
Can it be blameless? They expose his eyes:
Which look is guilty? They expose his brain:
it created a God. They expose the cleanest part of his breast,
they open up all his dreams, parade them one by one.
They expose his teeth, his tongue,
spitefully they expose his limbs under siege,
they yank butterflies from the terror of his belly,
they spit on the flesh of history, his lips,
and they show him the site: a hanging rope.
He hears a unanimous voice: "God has sent you this."
And not even a child's crying. Or a single tear.

Extraña juventud

   Hundir las manos en el agua
del tiempo. Ir al fondo
mismo del futuro que pasa.
Descender por sonidos
que antes nadie escuchara,
sabiendo que no existen
la vida y la esperanza.
Deshacer el ovillo
dentro del alma
desnudando a los mitos
con un golpe de luz en la mirada.
Vivir por vivir hoy,
no por vivir mañana.
Estar siempre en la punta
de polvo de la espada.
Beber despacio el tiempo
—el nuestro y nuestra nada—.
Acariciar de noche
las estrellas mojadas.
Y de día esos labios
en que el dolor se para
indicando que hay algo
extraño que no pasa.

Strange Youth

   Plunge your hands into the water
of time. Get to the very bottom
of the future passing.
Go down by sounds
nobody listened to before,
knowing that life and hope
don't exist.
Unravel the skein
within your soul
stripping the myths
with a blow of light in your eyes.
Live for today, live,
not for tomorrow.
Stand always on the sword's
point of dust.
Drink time slowly
—our time and our nothingness.
By night caress
soaked stars.
And by day those lips
on which pain stops,
that tell you something strange
is not happening here.

Querido hermano

Querido hermano:
Tenemos que olvidarte porque sentimos miedo
aunque todo está en orden desde que tú te fuiste.
Los padres hablan alto para borrar el sitio
de tu silencio. Todos
vamos elaborando nuestra muerte más seria
que tu vida, pues somos
más justos. Lo sabemos: todo el mundo lo dice.
Sólo yo pienso. Y dudo.
(Algunas veces siento la sangre dividida
imaginando un rostro no visto en el oriente:
el tuyo. Yo era entonces
muy niña y no recuerdo.)
Vivimos solitarios, sombras entre la niebla,
caminando detrás de la primera sombra,
levantando los brazos de las llagas del cuerpo,
con la mirada vuelta a ningún horizonte.
Un aire de silencio nos vela la palabra,
aunque tenemos todos permiso para el grito
que traspase la idea en que no estés borrado.

¿Qué fuego descubriste?
¿Qué secreto te envuelve por la casa?
Si algunas veces siento que me falta un pedazo
de la tierra que piso, de la sangre que llevo,
de una parte de Dios, extraña y silenciosa,
pienso si se habrá ido contigo por el mundo
dejándome este hueco en la frente perpleja.

Dear Brother

   Dear Brother:
We must forget you because we're afraid,
even though everything's under control since you went away.
Our parents talk loudly to erase the site
of your silence. We are all
constructing our death, much more serious
than your life, after all we're in the right.
We know it: everyone says so.
Only, I sit thinking. And doubting.
(Sometimes I feel my blood split
imagining a face unseen in the east:
yours. I was a child then
and I don't remember.)
We live in solitude, shadows in mist,
walking behind the first shadow,
raising our arms from the body's wounds,
with our eyes turned to a non-horizon.
An air of silence veils our speech,
though we all have permission to yell,
to pass through the idea you don't exist.

   What fire did you discover?
What secret shrouds you at home?
If sometimes I feel I lack a piece
of the earth I walk on, of the blood I bear,
of a part of God, strange and silent,
I ask if maybe it left with you into the world,
leaving me this hollow space to muddle my mind.

Diáspora

    Si supiera qué indican cuando me indican . . .
Quién puede asegurarme que no soy sólo un nombre,
quién puede hallarme, cierta, en los contornos
maltrechos de mi sombra.
Quién puede colocarme de pie sobre la tierra
y quitarme después, y que en el viento
permanezca mi orilla irreparable.
Qué dedo me bordea la boca, no el hastío.
No sé si son palabras o sueños lo que llevo,
ni quién es ese pájaro que oscuramente huye
cuando amanece. Ni qué recuerdo,
ni qué es lo que todos me dicen que recuerde.
Una mano aburrida me ha dejado en el suelo
—en camino de luces detectoras de alas;
arcillas fugitivas por los cielos vacíos—,
encadenada a un ansia de palabras prohibidas,
de palabras que esperan la señal para el grito
que devuelva los cuerpos a sus almas errantes.
Es como si entre todos estuvieran ocultas
y viviéramos una consigna de silencio,
solos y peregrinos entre aguas y nieblas
con las resecas sienes atravesando sombras,
esperando, esperando . . . Huyendo de los largos
reflectores que arrancan a Dios de su silencio.

Diaspora

If I knew what they point at when they point at me . . .
Who can guarantee that I am not just a name,
who can find me, for certain, in the battered ribs
of my shadow.
Who can put me feet flat on earth
and take me away later. And in the wind
would my marker remain unclaimed.
What finger traces my mouth, not boredom.
I don't know if I carry words or dreams,
or the name of that bird in dark flight
at dawn. Or what I remember,
or what it is everyone tells me I remember.
A bored hand left me on the ground
—traveling on light-detector wings;
fugitive clay through empty skies—
chained to a thirst for forbidden words,
words waiting for a signal, the cry
that returns bodies to their lost souls.
It's as if they were hidden in everyone
and we were living in an order of silence,
alone and wandering in water and mist,
bone dry temples crossing shadows,
waiting, waiting . . . Fleeing from the long
searchlights that drag God out of his silence.

Ved a un hombre

*"Una esperanza se ha ido del mundo, una soledad
ha comenzado para cada hombre libre". A.C.*

    Ved a este hombre.
La sombra de su cuerpo cubre todo el camino
y oscuros pájaros sin voz,
sin música, se estrellan, hojas solitarias,
a sus plantas. Lutos que giran
muy cerca de sus ojos arruinados,
de su mirada antigua que lucha contra el musgo
por seguir contemplando más belleza.
En su fondo se alzan
gestos purificados a través de los tiempos.
Mirad. No espanta
su postura de herido en pie, ahuyentando
los violentos plurales en acecho.
Pasa la cinta presurosa
de muchos que sonríen con labios estrenados,
agitando la ropa que en serie echaron fuera
de algún laboratorio, o sus gestos de slogan
—todos iguales. Como en un espejo—.
Y le dicen adiós con muecas, apretándose
las caderas impuras.
No, no. No espanta.
Dan deseos
de caer de rodillas,
de acariciar sus pies casi raíces
y su inocente sangre
antes que cualquier bota lo derribe.

To See a Man

> "One more hope has left the world; one more solitude
> has begun for every free man." A.C

    See this man.
The shadow of his body swallows the road whole,
and black birds without voice,
without music, like solitary leaves, crash
at his feet. Grief hovers
close to his ruined eyes,
to his worn gaze in struggle against the moss,
trying to keep on seeing more beauty.
Out of the depths gestures
rise up purified across time.
Look at him. There's no horror
in his wounded stance, scattering
violent impulses in ambush.
The film promptly passes around
those who smile with put-on lips,
shaking around clothes spewed out ready-made
from some laboratory, or hand signs like slogans
—all men are the same. Like mirrors—.
And they tell him goodbye with a grimace, squeezing
impure thighs.
No, no. No horror in him.
You want to fall
on your knees,
caress his feet nearly turned into roots,
his innocent blood,
before a boot, anyone's boot, knocks him flat.

En la orilla

　　Alguien dijo: Partir.
Partir . . . Partir . . .
Huir del polvo y de las alas,
de las arañas, de los látigos,
de las palabras, de los puños.
Huir entre algodones
sin oir los alambres ni los huesos.
Descender,
descender entre alas de aceite
—oh, los cuerpos de goma—,
apartando las uñas y los soplos.
Pasar. No estar. (¿En dónde
podría estar?) No estar.
No estar.

　　Se hundieron archipiélagos de estrellas.
Se helaron las hogueras en los montes.
Extensos vientos amarillos
arrancaron la flor definitiva.

On the Border

    Someone said: Leave.
Leave . . . Leave . . .
Run away from dust and wings,
spiders, whips,
words, fists.
Run away in dead silence,
don't listen to barbed wire or bones.
Go down,
go down on well-oiled wings
—oh, the slickness of bodies—
splitting fingernails and breaths.
Go on. Not to be. (Where
then?) Not to be.
Not to be.

Archipelagos of stars sank.
Mountain fires froze.
Long yellow winds
stripped the last flower.

(¿Existió alguna vez la flor?)
Esto fue siempre un desierto
de tormenta y ceniza.
Una mano extendida sobre el mundo.
El viento, un viento de tierras desiertas,
de continentes desolados,
que silbó entre los muertos,
la llenaba de polvo y de papeles.
(Los dedos fueron tibiamente blancos.
Después se le quedaron como pájaros yertos.)
Y nadie dijo: "Basta".
Se quedó sobre la llanura. (Dónde
podría estar.) Alambres retorcidos,
frío metal—el alma huyó—arrancado,
dispuesto para fuego, viento o lluvia.

Luego, un ser de otro tiempo,
cargó aquello en su carro
y se perdió por un camino.

(Did the flower ever exist?)
This was always a desert
of storms and ashes.
A hand hanging over the world.
The wind, a wind of desert lands,
of desolate continents,
that whistled among the dead,
filled it with dust and debris.
(Fingers were luke-warm whiteness.
Later, they were like stiff birds.)
And no one said: "That's enough."
It stayed on the plain. (Where
on earth . . . ?) Twisted wire,
cold metal—the soul fled—rooted up,
ready for fire, wind or rain.

Afterwards, a being from another time
loaded up all that in his cart
and vanished without a trace.

Sé que me roban algo

    Y todo este quedar sobre las playas,
para morirse un día.
Dicen que allí . . .
Pero respondo que vivo ahora.
Que es sobre esta tierra donde estoy,
en donde me conozco,
en donde estoy muriendo
un poco más a cada instante.
Sobre esta tierra que me roban,
sobre estos prados que me huelen
a muerte inhabitada.
Que debe ser aquí, en donde somos.
Que este vivir para la muerte
no es vivir humano. Nadie me hará creerlo.
Alguien me debe algo
que no estará en la muerte
y duerme sobre el pecho
estrellado del mundo.
Sé que en alguna parte
alguien me quiere débil
para domar mi sangre.
Para robarme esta
vida que exijo ahora,
para hacer de mí un cuerpo mortificado
y dulce
escondiéndome sombras
por detrás de la muerte.
Sé que me roban algo
y no sé quién, ni dónde.

I Know I'm Being Cheated

And all this lying about on the beach,
just to die one day.
They say that maybe over there . . .
But I say, I'm alive now.
It's here, on this earth, where I am,
where I know myself,
where I'm dying
a little more every second.
Of this earth I'm being cheated,
of these fields that smell like
deserted death.
It has to be here, where we are.
This living for death
isn't living, isn't human. No one can make me believe it.
Someone owes me something
that isn't inside death,
that sleeps upon the starry
breast of the world.
I know that somewhere,
someone wants me weak
to tame my blood.
To cheat me of this life
that I need now,
to make of me a sweetly
mortified body,
hiding shadows from me
behind death.
I know I'm being cheated.
I just don't know who, or where.

Respuesta a las brujas

    Comadres de mi pueblo,
brujas de cara, nidos de susurros,
echad agua bendita
en mi almohada. Sueño
que cada hueso mío reverdece
y se pone derecho y en su sitio
—con los ojos muy bien abiertos sueño,
oscuras brujas mías—,
junto a otro cuerpo que me da sentido;
y que algo como un soplo
—Dios no se enfada, brujas,
pero rezad por mí; por tanta dicha—,
me sube de los pies a la cabeza
quebrando mi cintura
en un nudo de llanto que no es llanto.
Hay algo que se para en no sé dónde,
tal vez en un paisaje
de quietos horizontes, y unos ojos
en silencio me miran.
Y es de dos todo el mundo.
Y esta naranja donde nos morimos
se sabrá someter a nuestra espalda.

Response for Witches

    Go ahead, my hometown crones,
witch-faces, whispering wasp nests,
throw your holy water
on my pillow. I dream
that every bone of mine grows green again,
is straight and whole
—with my eyes wide open I dream,
oh dark witches of mine—
next to that other body giving me life;
and that something like breath itself
—God's not angry, witches,
but pray for me anyway; for so much joy—
rises from my feet to my head,
shattering my waist
into a knot of weeping that isn't weeping.
There's something stops I'm not sure where,
maybe in a landscape
of quiet horizons, and eyes
in silence look at me.
And the world is made of twos.
And this orange where we're dying
must know how to submit to our backs turned.

Sonoras brujas mías,
alas negras en torno de los cielos,
piernas, labios de niños
rugen en vuestras venas.
Yo rezaré un responso por vosotras
—me contempláis en grupos de cadáveres
y os santiguáis . . . —. Mantengo
algo de la raíz y de la espuma,
de la nave y el viento que os reune
como a viejos papeles en el polvo
de esquinas sin sentido.
Vuestro diablo está por los estómagos.
Yo me miro en el agua de unos ojos
y me mido en un brazo
que me señala siempre hacia la vida.

Ear-splitting witches of mine,
black wings framing the skies,
the legs and lips of children
roar in your veins.
I will say a response for you
—you looking at me in clustered corpses,
crossing yourselves . . . —. I hold
some of the root and the wave,
the ship and the wind that sweep you together
like an old paper trail into dusty
scribbled corners.
Your devil is pitted deep in the belly.
I see myself in pools of eyes,
but my measure's always from an arm
that shows me the way toward life.

La trampa

Julia Uceda, qué has hecho de tu sombra.
Mujer sin huella, cuerpo
sin apellido,
denominas al humo, a las lluvias y al viento.
A todo lo que pase y se borre y se pierda.

Has buscado una voz por donde había
viejos mitos desiertos.
Has adorado dioses derribados
en hondos agujeros
y ahora todas las aguas de la tierra
lloran desde los montes por tu cuerpo
donde muere la muerte. Y donde muere
la vida al mismo tiempo.
Mujer con los brazos mojados
en el antiguo corazón de un cuento,
con las espaldas frente al Todo
y las pupilas derribando miedos,
las viejas madres-muertes harán rondas
para que pudra tu secreto,
y escuches en los muros de tu vientre
un golpear de pétalos y huesos
y graves caracoles masculinos
en las tardes de invierno.
Te rozarán la frente largas dudas
como ásperas lenguas de perro.
Escupirán inviernos en tu llama
porque has jugado con su fuego
y mostrarán de ti, cuando te vayas,
un helado cerebro.

The Trap

    Julia Uceda, what have you done with your shadow.
Woman with no prints, body
with no name,
yet you give names to smoke, to rain, to wind.
To everything alive that will be erased and lost.

    You've trailed a voice
of ancient deserted myths.
You've adored gods hurled
into deep gullies
and now all the waters of the earth
weep from the mountains for your body
where death dies. And where life
dies too.
Woman with arms soaked
in the ancient heart of story,
shoulders facing the universe
and pupils tearing down fear,
old mothers-old deaths will do the rounds
so your secret rots,
so you hear deep inside your belly
petals and bones being broken
and seashells, slow and stately,
on winter afternoons.
Long doubts, like the rough tongues of dogs,
will brush your brow.
They will spit winter on your flame
for playing with their fire
and when you're gone, they will exhibit you
with your frozen brain.

El otro umbral

     No me quiero caer entre los muertos.
Quiero ser un párpado frío,
luna callada por los hielos,
navegar sobre la noche
con ojos pálidos y eternos.
Mirar a un mismo tiempo todo
y resbalarme por el cielo
como una llama en Dios mojada
que va rodando y encendiendo.

Quiero seguir de cualquier modo.
No me quiero quedar en mis objetos
como el polvo que borra las estancias,
hecha espalda de luces y de espejos.

Y es que me voy quedando sola
rodeada por un silencio
que va mutilando mis pasos
y oscureciendo mi sendero.

No podré caminar un día.
Me pondrán sortija de hielo
para mis bodas con el musgo
en la catedral de los sueños.

Matada o muerta y no sé dónde
—como la gente de mi tiempo—
con un clamor de manos rotas
tendré que derrumbarme entre los muertos.

The Other Threshold

I don't want to fall among the dead.
I want to be a cold eyelid,
a moon silenced in ice,
to navigate the night
with pale, eternal eyes.
I want to see everything at once
and slide through the sky
like a flame dipped in God
cartwheeling sparks in space.

I want to go on no matter what.
I don't want to cling to my things
like the dust that wipes out rooms,
or turn into the other side of lights and mirrors.

I'm more and more alone, you see,
surrounded by silence
mutilating my footsteps
and darkening my path.

Soon I won't be able to walk.
They'll slip a ring of ice on me,
make me marry the moss
in the cathedral of dreams.

Murdered or plain dead, where I don't know,
—like people everywhere now—
with a clamor of broken hands
I'll drop, forced to fall among the dead.

From: *Sin mucha esperanza*

Invitación al país de los hombres

A través de mí, regresa.
Sea yo, hasta ti, tu camino.

Dame tu mano
y ven de nuevo entre nosotros.
Llega, en mi voz,
a tu destino externo.
Busca en mí
tus senderos perdidos,
el hogar y sus árboles,
el color de la tarde y los perfumes
de tu niñez. Los roperos amados
se abren, tal vez, en mis silencios
y un olor abrigado
se esparce en tu memoria.
                         Camina,
recorre de mi mano
tus ensueños inmóviles.
                      Háblame
de la caliente orilla de la infancia
y de la tierra oculta por la nieve
—se me ha olvidado el mar
y no sé nada. Créalo—.
                      Dime
si te gustaban las tormentas
o si jugabas a soldados.

Pasea por tu infancia nuevamente.
Así veré que has vuelto.

From: *Without Much Hope*

Invitation to the Country of Men

Through me, come back.
Let me be the way home to you.

Give me your hand
and come among us once again.
Find in my voice
your other destiny.
Look within me
for your lost tracks,
home, the trees,
the color of the afternoon and the scent
of your childhood. Beloved closets
seem to open into my silence
and a cloaked perfume
drifts through your memory.
                                      Come then,
let my hand sift
through your silent dreams.
                                      Speak to me
of the warm shore of childhood
and the land hidden by snow
—I've forgotten the sea
and know nothing. Create it for me.
                                      Tell me
if you used to like storms
or if you played soldier.

Wander through your childhood once again.
That way I'll know you have returned.

La extraña

> *"La fatiga è sedersi senza farse notare".*
> *Cesare Pavese:* Il vino triste

Me levanté sin que se dieran cuenta
y salí sin hacerme notar.
Había estado todo el día
entre ellos, intentando
hacerme oír,
procurando decirles
lo que me habían encargado.
Pero el recado que me dieron
no era preciso. El humo,
la música, el ruido de las risas
y de los besos—estallaban
como las rosas en el aire—,
eran más fuertes que mi voz. Cansada
de mi trabajo inútil,
me levanté,
abrí la puerta
y salí del hermoso lugar.
Desde la calle
miré por la ventana: nadie había
advertido mi ausencia.
Caminé. Volví el rostro:
ninguno me seguía.

The Stranger

"La fatiga è sedersi senza farse notare."
Cesare Pavese: Il vino triste

I got up without a word
and I left without a sign.
I had been with them
all day, trying
to be heard,
trying to tell them
what they had charged me with.
But the message they gave me
wasn't necessary. The smoke,
the music, the noise of laughter
and kisses—exploded
like roses in the air—
were stronger than my voice. Tired
of my useless labor,
I got up.
I opened the door
and left the lovely place.
From the street
I looked through the window: no one had
noticed my absence.
I walked. I turned my head:
no one was following me.

Diálogo

Aquí estoy—murmuró—. *Vengo a traerle
su libertad.* Sobre la mesa estaba
doblada con cuidado, limpia,
recién salvada. Alzó
su rostro hacia el jardín:
dulces barcos de humo
marchaban hacia el mar.

El mar . . . Ningún camino
podría conducirla. Todo era
una espiral interminable.

El dijo:
Te amaba . . . Te he amado . . . Ella
—tenía vueltos al jardín los ojos—
oyó: *yo temo.* Y sonreía
a los barcos que eran catedrales,
y luego montes y después rebaños
y al fin ya nada: sólo
una gran pesadumbre.

¿Qué temes?—dijo. Y su voz venía
del país de las sombras—*Oh, no,
no temas nada.* Y él: *No dije
"temo" sino "te amo".* Parecía
sorprendida. Miró
la libertad: sobre la mesa
ya no estaba. Recordó: *te amo . . .*

Alguien, una vez, dijo eso,
pero quién, cuándo, dónde . . .
No pudo
recordarlo. El esperaba su respuesta
y entonces, con dulzura,
se abrió la blusa y le mostró la muerte.

Dialogue

Here I am, she murmured. *I bring
freedom.* It was on the table,
folded with care, clean,
freshly salvaged. She raised
her face toward the garden:
sweet ships of smoke
sailed away toward the sea.

The sea . . . No road
could take her. It was all
an unending spiral.

He said:
I did love you . . . I loved you . . . She
—her eyes were turned to the garden—
heard: *I loathe.* And smiled
at ships that were cathedrals,
and then mountains, then flocks,
and finally nothing: only
a terrible grief.

What do you loathe?—she said. And her voice came
from shadowlands—*Oh, no,
please don't loathe me.* And he: *I didn't say
"I loathe" but "I love you".* She seemed
surprised, and looked
toward freedom: it was no longer
on the table, and remembered: *I love you . . .*

Someone said that, once,
but who, when, where . . .
She couldn't
remember. He waited for her reply,
so it was, gently,
she opened her blouse and showed him death.

Eterno oleaje

Será primero una ola niña
sobre la ciega playa. Luego
una delgada espuma persistente,
más tarde
un redoblar de todo el horizonte
que avanza, que se empuja
para tomar contacto con la orilla.

En cada grueso oleaje, en cada arruga
del mar, en cada ojo
de espuma por la arena
de fuego, estará un hombre
por él y por su extensa
cadena de fantasmas. Por las sombras
que no tuvieron cuerpo;
por todos
los que anulados vagan
sin país, sin sepulcro.

Con la memoria
de los que fueron olvidados
volverán: "Ya llegamos
a la patria". Y jamás
será la patria. Siempre
habrá otras olas, y anchos nudos,
gruesas crestas de mar. El hombre

Eternal Waves

First there'll be a little wave
upon the blind beach. Then
thin persistent foam,
later,
the horizon will rumble and roll,
advancing, pushing
to make contact with the shore.

In each thick wave, in each wrinkle
of the sea, in each eye
of foam, across the burning
sand, there will be a man
for himself and for his long
chain of ghosts. For the shadows
without bodies;
for all those who've been
annulled and who wander
without a country, without a grave.

With the memory
of those who were forgotten
they will return: "Now we've reached
our country." But it will never
be their country. There will always
be other waves, and wide knots,
the sea's thick cresting. The man

irá pisando playas
de fuego, rocas
que hirieron otros pies,
algas que se enredaron a otras plantas.
Caminará por siempre
—a través de paisajes con recuerdos—,
el sol contra su espalda
y una arruga profunda
en la frente horadada por el viento.

"¿Era esta mi patria?"
—preguntará de nuevo—.
Y pasando de largo,
como un extraño entre los ríos,
regresará a la orilla
de que partió—no la recuerda—
pidiendo paz para sus muertos.

will go on stepping on beaches
of fire, rocks
that wounded other feet,
algae entangled in other plants.
He will walk forever
—across remembered landscapes—
the sun against his back
a deep frown
on his forehead burrowed by the wind.

"Was this my country?"
—he will ask again.
And moving on,
like a stranger among rivers,
he will return to the shore
where he began—it is unremembered—
begging peace for his dead.

Elegía sobre el tiempo

I.

Alguien dirige
la circulación del Infierno.
No digáis
que de allí no se vuelve.
La arena
todo lo modifica: todo
lo iguala. Pero siempre
ha de haber condenados.
Conozco
a los reos del hombre
y a los absueltos en sábado.
Con frecuencia vi el rostro
de los fieles a la contradicción,
de los abrazados
a la inseguridad. En el crujido
de la madera,
durante noches y silencios,
adiviné en el peso de los huecos vacíos
toda su queja y su protesta muda
por tener incrustado entre sus dientes
un cristo de diamante.
El fuego,
abrasando sus lenguas,
iluminaba otra verdad, más honda,
que decir no podían.
Yo, una más entre ellos,
los oí protestar
por el fraude en cuyas frías aras
su sangre había corrido
y correrá la mía.

Elegy Over Time

I.

Someone controls
the circulation of Hell.
Don't tell me
you can't come back from there.
The sands
change everything: make everything
the same. But the condemned
are always here.
I know
who is accused by men
and who absolved on sabbath.
I grew used to seeing faces
faithful to contradiction,
faces embracing
insecurity. In the creaking
of wood,
over nights and silence,
I divined in those hollow spaces
all the weight of their complaint, their mute protest,
because incrusted in their teeth
there was a diamond christ.
The fire,
burning their tongues,
kindled another truth, much deeper,
one they couldn't say.
I, one more among them,
heard their protest fall
on the lies, on the cold altar,
saw their blood run
just as mine will run.

II.

Perdida entre todos
espero el regreso de los condenados.
Los labios entonan himnos ya tardíos
y el suelo se cubre de mirtos y rosas
que habrán de pisar los pies imposibles.
Banderas, incienso, palomas con frío,
solos y con frío se mueven sin rumbo.
Y como si alguien corriera una vela
cae de algún lado un raro silencio
y cruza una extensa presencia invisible
que llena las luces de sombra y apaga
los rostros y el día. En vano pensamos
que nosotros no fuimos los jueces.

III.

Los reos no miran a un lado ni a otro.
Sus ojos contemplan la muerte en que yacen
—niños que dejaran la cuna con sueño—.

Tú, que cortaste la leña del bosque
con el hacha indignada del justo;
tú, que trajiste la llama y el aire y los lienzos;
tú, que pusiste la firma y el sello de sangre en un lado

II.

Lost in the crowds
I wait the return of the condemned.
Lips intone belated hymns
and the ground is covered in myrtle and roses
for impossible feet to walk on.
Flags, incense, shivering doves,
alone and shivering, move adrift.
And as though someone dropped a sail,
a rare silence falls from somewhere
and a larger, invisible presence passes,
filling the lights with shadow, blacking out
faces and days. Useless to think
that we were not judges.

III.

The accused look neither right nor left.
Their eyes see the death they lie in
—like children leaving the cradle, still sleepy.

You who cut wood in the forest
with the angry axe of the just;
you who brought flame, air, and canvas;
you who put your signature and the seal of blood
                                        [on one side

del papel y decías salvar a las vírgenes,
a las castas esposas y jóvenes madres
que al llegar su otoño,
una a una rindieron tributo a la sombra, al polvo y al sueño,
decid: ¿habéis visto estos rostros? ¿Conocéis
que son muertos y nada podrá devolverles la carne
ni la luz con que amaban? ¿No veis que los himnos
no borraron jamás la derrota, el temor y la muerte
ni el exilio del mar y los pájaros?

Los reos no miran a un lado ni a otro:
nada pueden mirar los que vieron la sombra.
En vano pensamos
que nosotros no fuimos los jueces.

IV.

La muerte, en la verde cornisa del templo, sonríe,
y sus palmas imitan el gesto de aplauso del hombre en la calle.
(Las arenas suavizan cualquier desnivel de la historia.)
Y como en los cuentos,
los que ya perdonaron regresan
al calor de sus tibios hogares y en ocios de sábado
procrearán a los reos futuros
que serán condenados en lunes.

of the paper and claimed you were saving virgins,
faithful wives and young mothers,
who with the coming of autumn, their autumn,
one by one paid tribute to shadow, dust and sleep,
tell me: Have you seen these faces? Do you know
they are dead and nothing can give back their flesh
or the light of their loving? Don't you see that hymns
can never wipe out defeat, fear and death,
can never wipe out the exile of sea and birds?

The accused look neither right nor left:
Those who've seen shadows can see nothing.
Useless to think
that we were not judges.

IV.

Death, up in the green cornice of the temple, smiles,
and his palms mime the gesture of applause of the man
                                                [in the street.
(The sands soften any differences in the story.)
And like a story,
those who readily forgave return
to the heat of their lukewarm homes, and on a lazy Saturday
they'll make the bodies of tomorrow's accused,
and these will be condemned on Monday.

Una patria se ve desde la cumbre

Lo que os voy a decir es como un grito.
Y es urgente esta forma entrecortada
—para que oigáis los golpes
de un corazón oculto—
porque responde a una pregunta
que no sé si me han hecho.

No puedo precisar en dónde
comenzó todo: hace edades o siglos
(siglos o edades
de irrompibles silencios).
Para mí sobrevino
en un lugar inesperado:
París, mil novecientos
cincuenta y nueve. La frontera
me había desnudado de la firme
protección de la patria
y sus conceptos nunca comprobados.
Ya no tenía
visillos de humo
para mis ojos: Carlos V
murió efectivamente; Don Quijote
era un libro
hermoso. Yo vivía, por fin,
no en el pasado, no
sobre el colchón de plumas
amargas, sino
en París mil novecientos
cincuenta y nueve.
Ardían
mis ojos nuevos, arrasados
de un aire de otro mundo.
Inesperadamente había
encontrado mi tiempo.

A Country Seen From Afar

What I am going to tell you is like a scream.
This rough-cut form is urgent:
—it's so you can hear the pounding
of a hidden heart—
because it responds to a question
I'm not sure they've even asked me.

I can't be precise where
it all began: maybe ages or centuries ago
(centuries or ages
of unbreakable silence).
For me it came
in a place, suddenly:
Paris, nineteen hundred
and fifty nine. The border
stripped me of the firm
protection of my country
and her untested ideas.
I no longer had
curtains of smoke
for eyes: Charles V
was really dead; Don Quixote
was a lovely
fancy. I was living, finally,
not in the past, not
on a stinging featherbed,
but
in Paris nineteen hundred
and fifty nine.
My new eyes
burned, demolished
by the air of another world.
Suddenly I had
found my time.

Allí, en París, vi
por primera vez al enemigo
de Don Quijote,
de toda la cultura
occidental. No hablaba
como en el cine
de mi país.
    Su voz
me recordaba aquellas otras voces
que levantaron Grecia.
Su rostro, rudo,
puro, de campesino cordobés
y su viejo uniforme (había
olvidado decir que la película
narraba una sencilla historia
rural,
de la última guerra),
velaban por completo
sus oscuros propósitos
contra mí—contra el espíritu
occidental y sus valores
eternos ... —. Sólo
supe la historia de un soldado,
de su hogar entre campos
de trigo— ¿Ucrania? ¿Andalucía?—,
de su madre, arropada en lutos
y viuda como
las mujeres de Lorca.

For the first time, there in Paris
I saw the enemy
of Don Quixote,
of western culture,
all of it. And he didn't speak
like the movies
from my country.
                      His voice
made me remember those other voices
who built Greece.
His face, rough,
pure like a Cordoban peasant,
and his old uniform (I
forgot to say that the film
told a simple country
story,
from the last war),
completely veiled
his darker design
against me—against the western
mind and its eternal
values... I saw
only the story of a soldier,
of his home amid fields
of wheat—the Ukraine? Andalusia?—
of his mother, dressed in mourning,
widowed
like Lorca's women.

                    Si me hubiese
tapado los oídos; si la lengua,
extraña, melodiosa,
se hubiera dejado de oír, aquella dulce
historia, aquel
paisaje, los soldados,
rotos, alegres,
habrían sido
los de la patria; aquellas
estaciones, del trayecto
desde Sevilla a Córdoba,
no de Ucrania, no
de donde fuesen.
                    Y aquel amor
entre dos seres casi niños,
habría merecido
un 1 a la censura.
                    No podía
a través de la húmeda cortina
de mis ojos, adivinar
los oscuros propósitos
contra mí.
                    Entonces más que nunca supe
que no era libre;
que nunca nadie
había sido libre.

If I had
covered my ears; if I hadn't heard
the language,
strange and musical, that touching
story,
that landscape, those soldiers,
wasted yet happy,
could have been
my countrymen; those train
stations, the distance
from Seville to Cordova,
not the Ukraine, or
wherever it was. And that love
between a pair of kids,
would have earned
the censor's 1.
I couldn't
divine, through the wet curtain
of my eyes,
the dark design
against me. Then more than ever I knew
I wasn't free;
that no one ever
had been free.

             Si yo fuera
filósofo extraería
consecuencias, tal vez heterodoxas,
sobre el dolor del mundo, sobre
cierto pecado del mundo y algo
no sólo del país que vi desde la cumbre,
sino del hombre contra el hombre.
Probablemente haría
un estudio científico
de ciertos individuos
borrachos de poder.
                    Y es posible que entonces
hubiésemos llegado
a la raíz del pacto de silencio
entre los siglos.
              Puede
que entonces comprendiéramos
que la manzana sigue y sigue
rodando sobre
nuestras cabezas erguidas de
miembros de la cultura
occidental.
           Pero eso
tal vez no es cosa mía. Os cuento
en forma de poema, un poco
entrecortadamente para
que oigáis los golpes
de un corazón oculto,
esto que sobrevino
contra mí
en un lugar inesperado:
París, mil novecientos
cincuenta y nueve. Era
mirar desde una cumbre
una imposible patria.

                    If I were
a philosopher, I would draw
conclusions, unorthodox ones maybe,
about the pain of the world,
about the sin of the world, and something
not only about the country I saw from afar,
but about man against man.
I'd probably do
a scientific study
of certain individuals
drunk with power.
                    It's even possible that
then we might have dug
out of the centuries the root of the pact of silence.
                    Maybe then
we'd understand
that the apple rolls and rolls
and rolls
over our heads proudly raised
on the limbs of Western
culture.
                    But maybe that's no business
of mine. I tell you this
in the form of a poem, a little
rough-cut,
so you can hear the pounding
of a hidden heart,
this thing that came
against me
in a place, suddenly:
Paris, nineteen hundred
and fifty nine. It was
like seeing from afar
an impossible country.

Cumpleaños

> *"Con frecuencia me detengo, asombrada, ante*
> *esa cosa increíble que me sirve de rostro".*
> Simone de Beauvoir: La fuerza de las cosas

Desde el espejo
me mira agazapada, jugueteando
con los ovillos y los pájaros.
Nada la distrae de su espera:
los ojos en mis ojos,
acecha mis motivos
de repulsa, y exhibe
su derecho a quedarse en los espejos.
Soy un ovillo más, uno más . . .

Y juega:
simula una batalla que no existe;
o en su rostro de arena
dibuja gestos de vencida. Inútil
alarma.
Pero soy su victoria diferente.

Si voy sin detenerme. Si
no me aparto, ni huyo. Si
digo *sí* y es *sí* y *bueno* . . .
o *como quieras*, y me es igual ya todo
—o *todo es nada*—, ¿cómo
puedo ser su victoria?

Birthday

> *"Often I stop, astonished, before this*
> *incredible thing that is called my face."*
> Simone de Beauvoir: The Force of Things

From the mirror
she looks at me, crouching, toying
with skeins and birds.
Nothing distracts her from the waiting:
her eyes on my eyes,
she spies on my motives
for refusal, and exhibits
her right to remain enmirrored.
I am one more ball of yarn, one more . . .

And she plays:
she simulates a non-existent battle
or in her face of sand
she draws gestures of defeat. Useless
alarm.
But I am her other victory.

If I go without dawdling. If
I stick close, don't go. If
I say *yes* and it is *yes* and *good* . . .
or *as you please,* and it's all the same to me
—or *everything* is *nothing*—how
can I be her victory?

Si por ninguna gota de mi sangre
se ha perdido un triunfo. Si
nunca nada dijo *sí* para mi oído. Si
sí es para mí *no* y *nada*
es *todo* siempre, ¿cómo
me espera, hora tras hora, día
a día, a mí?

Admiro su grandeza
sin causa y el tesón
de sus ojos inmóviles y atentos
sobre los pálidos caminos
que no invitan a huir.

Si supiera
que he dejado las armas,
y que miro, curiosa, los crepúsculos
hasta ese, que funda
en el uno total las dos imágenes.

If no triumph has been lost
for a single drop of my blood. If
nothing ever said *yes* to my ear. If
yes is for me *no* and *nothing*
is always *everything*, how is it
she waits for me, hour after hour, day
after day?

I admire her greatness
without a cause and the tenacity
of her eyes, fixed and staring
on pale roads
that are not an invitation to flight.

If she only knew
that I have left off weapons,
that I look at twilight, bemused,
even this one fusing
into a total oneness two images.

"No Trespassing"

Nadie dirá: "Murió otra Julia Uceda"
porque su cuerpo pasa todavía
entre nosotros. Porque se sienta y habla.
Nadie dirá: "¿Por qué? . . . "
                                      Distraídamente
cualquiera puede—si se roza
a otro sin querer, sin advertirlo—
quedarse con la vida entre los dedos.
Y ya después
sólo se vive muerte— ¿todos
vivimos muerte? ¿Ese
era el secreto de la vida?—: doce
horas de muerte sin contar insomnios,
expulsados del tiempo, sobre altas
rocas de soledad.
Y acumulamos
a los pequeños muertos de la infancia,
al perdido desván en donde duermen
objetos que ya nadie usará nunca
ni manos pulirán dándole vida,
otro cadáver más: como una hoja
que un ausente dejó dentro del libro
cerrado para siempre.
Y nadie sabe cómo
se llamará la vida entre los muertos.

No Trespassing

No one will say: "Some other Julia Uceda died"
because her body still walks
among us. Because she sits and talks.
No one will say: "Why? ... "
                                       Without thinking,
anyone can—if you brush against
someone without meaning to, without noticing—
walk off with somebody's life in your hands.
And then afterward,
you live only death—do we all
live death? Was that
the secret of life? Twelve
hours of death, without counting insomnia,
expelled from time, on the high
rocks of solitude.
So we accumulate
the small deaths of childhood,
the lost attic where objects
that nobody will ever use again sleep,
nor will hands polish one more corpse,
giving it life: like a leaf
that someone long gone left inside a book
closed forever.
And no one knows what
life is called among the dead.

From: *Poemas de Cherry Lane*

Noroeste

Si intentara decirlo
no sabría: el tiempo
y el espacio jugaban
una danza en el tronco de los árboles.

Cómo poner en su lugar
—tiempo y espacio—lo innombrable:
el vacío. No el *vacío* que está en el *Diccionario*,
definido y concreto,
sino el real, el otro, el sin palabras.
Ese que ni parece una palabra. Que no tiene
ni siquiera un idioma, una música, un gesto.

Inútil intentarlo. Sólo puedo
decir *tiempo* y *espacio*, mas no todo.
(Nunca se llega al fondo. Ni uno sabe
quién muere cuando entierran nuestro nombre.)

Era un reloj de manos rotas
que se dejó los dedos entre nubes,
sobre la mar—oh, sí: lo femenino,
lo múltiple y sin forma que da formas,
que devora y genera; la mar, Jorge Manrique,
que no pudiste ver cual yo veía—.

From: *Cherry Lane Poems*

Northwest

If I tried to say it,
I wouldn't know how: time
and space were doing
a dance on the trunks of trees.

How do you put in their place
—time and space—the unnameable:
the void. Not the *void* that's in the *Dictionary*,
defined and concrete,
but the real one, the other one, without words.
That doesn't even seem a word. That doesn't even have
language, music, gesture.

Useless to try it. I can only
say *time* and *space*, but not everything.
(You never get to the heart. You don't even know
who dies when they bury our names.)

It was a clock with broken hands,
fingers left among the clouds,
over the sea—oh yes: the feminine,
the multiple and formless that gives forms,
that devours and generates; the sea, Jorge Manrique,
that you couldn't imagine the way I did.

Y por ese reloj, sola, rampante,
con alas sí, con júbilos y alas,
yo, lo inútil, creyendo
un mensaje en mis manos poderosas.

Qué importaba el reloj, la mutilada
hora tradicional, los asaltados
espacios interiores donde el miedo
lloró sobre sí mismo replegado. Qué importaba
si yo tenía manos, huesos, júbilos
que entregar por respuesta . . .

El espacio era claro, pero luego
supo a cristal—no sé decirlo—,
a suelo huyendo.
A soledad callada y no sonora.

Y una mujer andaba, andaba, andaba.
Y era yo y no era yo, porque ya todo
era igual a sí mismo y sólo había
asido sombras y abrazado sombras.

No, dolor no, mas no podría
precisar . . . sino luces
hirientes de quirófanos.
Sí, vacíos también, todo vacío.
Todo hueco—futuros y pasados—:
un escalón de menos, un espacio
sin aire . . . No sabría
—ya lo advertí—decirlo.

And because of that lone, raging clock,
with wings yes, with rejoicing and wings,
I, how useless, believing
I had a message in my powerful hands.

What did the clock matter, the mutilated
traditional hour, the assaulted
inner spaces where fear
wept hunched over itself. What did it matter,
if I still had hands, bones, joy
to give for an answer . . .

The space was clear, but later
it tasted of crystal—I don't know how else to say it—
of the ground fleeing.
Of quiet, muted solitude.

And a woman walked and walked and walked.
And it was me and not me, because now everything
was the same and I had only
grasped shadows and embraced shadows.

No, pain no, though I can't be
precise . . . but blinding
lights of operating rooms.
Yes, empty too, all empty.
All hollow—all the futures and pasts—
one less step, a space
without air . . . I wouldn't know how
—I already told you—to say it.

Broadway, una noche

Aquella noche, Charlie,
qué sueño tan raro ... O tal vez no era un sueño.
La vida juega con sus planos
sin saber que medimos
el tiempo, que hemos dado
un orden. O lo sabe
y se burla. Lo tira por lo alto
y los naipes resbalan
de lo azul a la tierra ...

Al compás de una música que nadie
oyó jamás, danzaba: trozo
de papel en el viento.
Sin peso, sin medida, sin tiempo, en el espacio
infinito, danzaba ... ¿O no danzaba y eran
el cielo y la ciudad quienes seguían
la extraña música en su giro?

¿Qué luces, cuáles eran
las estrellas: las calles luminosas
—un río de cristal ardiente, Charlie—,
huyendo en todas direcciones,
o los ojos profundos, enigmáticos,
que eternamente parpadean?

¿Era Marte—oh, ya sé que no podría
ser—esa gota roja, arriba
—o abajo—quien lloraba
sangre o era Broadway gritando
sus misterios, sus secas
muertes desconocidas?

Broadway, One Night

That night, Charlie,
what a strange dream . . . Or maybe it wasn't a dream.
Life plays with the charts,
doesn't know that we measure
time, we've given
an order to things. Or knows it
and mocks us. Throws it up in the air
and the cards slip,
azur to earth . . .

I was dancing to the beat of music
no one ever heard: scrap
of paper in the wind.
Without weight, without measure, without time,
 in infinite
space, I was dancing . . . Or maybe I wasn't dancing and it was
the sky and the city who were following
the strange, twisting music?

Which were the lights,
the stars: the luminous streets
—a river of burning crystal, Charlie—
fleeing in all directions,
or the eyes, deep-sunk and cryptic,
eternally blinking?

Was that Mars—oh, I know it couldn't
be—that red drop, above
—or below—who was weeping
blood or was that Broadway screaming
its mysteries, its dry,
unknown deaths?

Sobre un río de trenes o bisontes,
sobre un rumor de selvas dominadas
por cristal y cemento; sobre cráneos
y totems; sobre el níquel,
sobre el mármol de Paros, yo danzaba,
cruzaba por la extensa
música del ardiente
templo.

   Abajo y muy lejana
Notre Dame agitaba su pañuelo
y Burgos y León me despedían:
sus piedras húmedas lloraban
—o no lloraban y era que la luna
les prestaba su brillo para el acto—
y en los sepulcros olvidados huesos
se hundían más y más . . .

Qué extraño sueño, Charlie . . . Los tejados
se poblaban de flores que venían
desde el mar y brotaban
de sus vientres de púrpura y acero
leves cuerpos que al punto
se entretejían por las escaleras
—perdidos ya, perdidos sin remedio—,
de hierro, por las firmes
tuberías del mundo.

Over a river of trains or bison,
over a riotous jungle ruled
by glass and cement; over skulls
and totems; over nickel,
over marble from Paros, I was dancing,
moving across the long
music of the blazing
temple.

   Below and very far away,
Notre Dame was waving her hanky
and Burgos and Leon were saying goodbye to me:
their damp stones were weeping
—or weren't weeping and it was the moon
lending a spotlight to the act—
and in their graves forgotten bones
were sinking more and more . . .

What a strange dream, Charlie . . . The rooftops
were peopled with flowers that came
from the sea and blooming
from their bellies of purple and steel
frail bodies that on the instant
were woven into stairways
—lost now, lost without a prayer—
of iron, into the solid
pipelines of the world.

¿Adónde irían, Charlie? ¿Pueden ellos,
sin sueños medievales, sin mis dioses
y mitos, sentir miedos? ¿Y qué clase
de miedos? La serpiente
no es la misma . . . Giraba,
yo giraba . . . Entendía
el orden.

   A mil metros
sobre el nivel del mar las caracolas
de metal, los pianos,
los oboes imponían
su ley, su fuerza inmensa
sobre el cristal y el níquel,
sobre León y Burgos, sobre mí . . . Se agitaba
la ciudad como un pecho
que respira.

   A mil metros
sobre el mar—sobre Grecia—
los oboes, los violines, los tibios saxofones
entonaban su himno de agonía.

Where do they go, Charlie?
Without the old dreams, without my gods
and myths, can they feel fear? And what kind
of fear? The serpent
is not the same one . . . I kept turning,
and turning . . . I was understanding
order.

   A thousand feet
above sea level metallic
conches, pianos,
oboes were exacting
their law, their immense force
over crystal and nickel,
over Leon and Burgos, over me . . . the city
heaved like a living
breast.

   A thousand feet
above the sea—above Greece—
oboes, violins, mellow saxes,
intoned their hymn of agony.

Mil metros por encima del mar, del Coliseo,
una pálida Roma
agitaba su mano, dulce mano
extranjera en la noche, despidiéndome
en su profundo y desdeñoso sueño.

Mil metros . . . A mil metros
sobre el nivel del mar el rubio líquido
de los delgados clarinetes, las ortigas
ardientes del tambor,
los oboes, los violines, las roncas y agrias voces
rompían, desgarraban
las noches amplias como rosas
oscuras con su himno
de agonía y de gloria
— ¡y cuántas muertes dentro!—
en sacrificio sobre el ara inmensa
de la ciudad: garganta
que profería un grito luminoso
cuajado de pequeñas
gargantas
esclavizadas o glorificadas
como Orfeo en su éxtasis.

Porque, Charlie, ¿quién podría decirlo?

Y yo danzaba
sin detenerme nunca: trozo
de papel en el viento.
Un papel donde alguien, distraído,
escribió algo y lo borró una lluvia.

A thousand feet above the sea, above the Coliseum,
a pale Rome
was waving her hand, her sweet hand
foreign in the night, saying goodbye to me
in her deep, disdainful sleep.

A thousand feet . . . A thousand feet
above sea level the liquid amber
of thin clarinets, the burning
nettles of the drum,
the oboes, the violins, the harsh, sour voices
were breaking, tearing apart
the nights plush as dark
roses with their hymns
of agony and glory
—and how many deaths inside!—
in sacrifice on the immense altar
of the city: a throat
uttering a luminous cry
crammed with smaller
throats
enslaved or glorified
like Orpheus in ecstasy.

But, Charlie, who can say all this?

And I was dancing,
never stopping: scrap
of paper in the wind.
A paper where someone, absentmindedly,
wrote something and the rain rubbed it out.

Rosas del sur

Las rosas del sur tienen una lágrima
a punto de caer. Charlie, las rosas . . .
Y ese vals demasiado
cursi tal vez. Las rosas, Charlie,
de Europa, que no has visto.

Cuando yo digo "rosas
del sur", en Alabama
piensas tal vez . . . En los violentos
ramos de rosas rojas, negras . . .
O en Pasadena . . . O quizá en esa rosa
perdida por tu infancia, que alguien trajo
y puso en una copa ya olvidada,
el lado de una Biblia dominical. Y hueles
a maderas antiguas.

Cuando yo digo "rosas
del sur" hay un revuelo
de tenues faldas por jaspeados mármoles,
un violín en la niebla, un Archiduque
en Austria: en una Europa
de antes del catorce . . .
(una Europa perdida, un Schöbrum muerto),
sepultada en un ritmo
violento de cañones y metralla.

Después Apollinaire con su cabeza
de algodón: herido por los siglos
de los siglos en todos los retratos.

Todos han muerto, Charlie.
Pero los valses quedan. Y Strauss.
Ahora, nosotros
somos vivos, reales.

Southern Roses

The roses of the South hold a tear
about to fall. The roses, Charlie . . .
And that waltz, too
too kitsch perhaps. The roses
of Europe, Charlie, that you haven't seen.

When I say "Southern
roses," you think maybe
of Alabama . . . Of violent
boughs of red and black roses . . .
or of Pasadena . . . Or maybe of that rose
lost in your childhood, that someone brought
and placed in a vase long forgotten, or
the border of a Sunday Bible. The scent
of old wood is in you.

When I say "Southern
roses," there's a whirl
of gauzy gowns through jaspered marble,
a violin in the mist, an Archduke
in Austria: in a Europe
before 1914 . . .
(A lost Europe, a dead Schöbrum),
buried in the rough
rhythms of canon and grapeshot.

Later, Apollinaire with his head
full of cotton: wounded for eternity
in all the portraits.

They've all died, Charlie.
But the waltz remains. And Strauss.
And we
are alive, real.

Yo, viva y verdadera, oigo contigo
esas "rosas del sur". De cualquier sur, amigo.

Sé que estoy viva
porque el espejo dice mi manera
de pintarme los labios,
de ordenar mi cabello.

Y escuchando esas rosas, esos valses
—todos brillantes, todos agitados
como suaves alientos,
muertos también, tras de los abanicos—
esperé que llamase
a mi puerta . . . al teléfono.
      Toda la tarde, como
      si no hubiese distancias
      ni palabras de hierro.

Ahora,
muy lentamente,
retardando el momento,
desordeno mi pelo y lo cepillo
pensando no sé qué, en otra cosa;
desprendo mis pendientes
y el rouge para dormir.

Los valses, Charlie,
hacen que vea en el espejo
las extrañas visitas de una casa en que alguien
espera, el grito
de un pájaro, el presente
de algún aniversario.
Mas ¿de qué aniversario?

Alive and real, I hear, like you,
those "Southern roses." From any South, friend.

I know that I'm alive
because the mirror names my way
of coloring my lips,
combing my hair.

And hearing those roses, those waltzes
—all brilliant, all flutter
like soft breaths,
dead too, behind the fans—
I waited for someone to call
at my door . . . on the telephone.
        All afternoon, as
        if there were no distances
        or iron words.

Now,
very slowly,
putting off the moment,
I mess up my hair and brush it
thinking I don't know what, something;
I take off my earrings
and then my makeup before going to bed.

The waltzes, Charlie,
make me see in the mirror
strange visitors to a house where someone
waits, the cry
of a bird, the present
of some anniversary.
But what anniversary?

No sé, Charlie . . . Los valses . . .
Toda esa Europa muerta me hizo
pensar que había una lágrima
a punto de caer desde las rosas
del sur . . . Y que yo estaba
viva—vivir es esperar—y que ninguna
lágrima iba a caer sobre mi hombro.
Pero ha caído . . .

Si otra vez digo "rosas
del sur" serán de Pasadena.
Si "olas", del Pacífico . . .
"Emperador", serpientes emplumadas
de Moctezuma . . . Schöbrum . . .
el gran teocalli con olor a sangre
y a metralla también. Y también muertos.

Porque todos han muerto, Charlie,
y sólo quedan valses y ruinas.
Las ruinas de piedra y las de carne.
Siempre serán la misma
rosa la de Alabama y la de Austria.

I don't know, Charlie . . . the waltzes . . .
Europe, dead Europe, made me
think there was a tear
about to fall from the roses
of the South . . . And that I was
alive—to live is to hope—and that no
tear was going to fall on my shoulder.
But it has fallen . . .

If I say "Southern roses"
once more, they'll be from Pasadena.
If I say "waves," from the Pacific . . .
"Emperor," the plumed serpents
of Montezuma . . . Schöbrum . . .
the great teocalli with the smell of blood
and grapeshot too. And the dead.

Because they've all died, Charlie,
and only the waltzes and ruins remain.
The ruins of stone and flesh.
Rose of Alabama, rose of Austria:
always the same rose.

Condenada al silencio

Para Ramón Sender

Nada más natural que estos paisajes
y esta luz en mi mesa y esta casa
—posible ya que se ha perdido todo—
y este extraño país en el que estoy.

Nada más natural que los nombres que oigo,
nada más natural que la nieve que cae,
la cama donde duermo,
los caminos que anduve . . .

Nada más natural. Nada más misterioso.

Aún no veo el conjunto
de todos los enigmas.
Sólo tengo fragmentos
amargos, disparates
de mí: gran disparate. O verdad honda.

Lo nuevo es la costumbre.
Lo acostumbrado olvido.
¿Soy otra? ¿Soy la misma? Los espejos
reflejan a una niña que se va y a una anciana
que blancamente llega,
pero nunca responden.
La respuesta está al filo:
cuando ya nada importa y no regresa el hombre.

Condemned to Silence

For Ramón Sender

Nothing more natural than these landscapes
and this light over my table and this house
—possible since everything's lost—
and this strange country in which I live.

Nothing more natural than the names I hear
nothing more natural than the snow that falls,
the bed where I sleep,
the roads I've walked . . .

Nothing more natural. Nothing more mysterious.

I still don't see all the sides
of every enigma.
I only have bitter
fragments, my own
folly: enormous folly. Or deep truth.

The new becomes the customary.
The habitual I forget.
Am I somebody else? Am I the same? Mirrors
reflect a child going away and an old woman
coming in whiteness,
but they never respond.
The answer is on the cusp:
when nothing matters anymore and a man does not return.

Pero entre tanto hay músicas
y luz en las estancias y retratos
—y horas que pasan esperando oír voces—
que miran desde ayer. Y también son misterio.

Habría que marcharse.
No haber venido nunca
porque el hondo misterio no está en los escalones
que bajamos; se agita
mortal y eterno en nuestro lado izquierdo,
y estamos impacientes porque amamos
lo que no debe amarse
ni ser amado quiere.

Yo me pregunto ahora,
en este pozo hondísimo,
si aún me quedan más pozos,
cuántos pozos me quedan
y hasta dónde el misterio será, como hasta ahora
natural, cotidiano
y si un día, en mis nieves,
no sentiré ya nada:
¡qué vergüenza, Dios mío!

Y digo que me quiero
marchar.
Que el juego es sucio,
que yo nada comprendo y que no hay paraísos
terrestres ni celestes. Sólo noches y noches
y una lenta caída del insomnio a la nada:
desde un sueño a otro sueño.

But meanwhile there is music
and light in the rooms and in the portraits
—and the passing hours hoping to hear voices—
with yesterday's gaze. And they too are a mystery.

It's really time to leave.
Better not to have come
because deep mystery isn't in the stairs
we go down; it flutters
mortal and eternal on our left side,
and we are impatient because we love
what ought not to be loved,
what wants not to be loved.

I ask myself now
in this deepest of wells,
if I still have more wells,
how many more wells are left to me
and how far the mystery goes, as up to now
it's been natural, every day,
and if one day, covered in whiteness,
I'll no longer feel anything:
God, how awful!

I tell you I want
to get out.
It's a dirty game,
and I don't understand anything and there's no paradise
on heaven or earth. Only nights and more nights,
and insomnia slowly dropping into the void:
going from dream to dream.

Lo más limpio es marcharse:
no dejar que se ensucie
nuestra mano inocente. Pero suena el teléfono
y *Sí, yo soy*, decimos
a las voces extrañas que, siempre equivocadas
de número, en la niebla
a cenar nos invitan.

Todo tan natural. Todo tan misterioso.

Cada hombre, en su noche,
sin saber dónde echarse como un perro,
descuelga los teléfonos, acude
a la cena, sostiene
hermosas copas de cristal: decora
un friso monstruoso. Sigue.

Nada más natural. Lo extraño es esto:
no poder derrumbarse en las aceras
porque hay que mantener el orden público.

The decent thing is to go away:
not to let our innocent hands
be dirtied. But the telephone rings
and *Yes, it's me*, we say
to strange voices (always a wrong
number), inviting us to dinner,
in the fog.

Everything so natural. Everything so mysterious.

Every man, in his own darkness,
not knowing where to lie down like a dog,
picks up the telephone, hurries off
to dinner, holds
beautiful crystal goblets: and decorates
a monstrous frieze. Goes on.

Nothing more natural. What's strange is this:
when you can't collapse on the sidewalk
because order must be maintained in public.

Nada se oye

¿Estuve sola
a través de los tiempos y los grupos
dorados del otoño; a través de la sombra
del árbol en el agua
inquieta o dura, y más y más allá?

¿Fui—fuimos—hablando entre la niebla
que fingía triunfantes
contornos a mi lado: un rostro puro,
muy extraño en su noche, con los signos
de un idioma remoto en su frente, en su boca?

Yo ¿le hablaba a la niebla y a la sombra
o es que alguien me oía?

¿Oía alguien?

La respuesta ¿era una voz o el viento?
Era una voz ¿o el agua
salvaje de ese río cruel y poderoso
que el amor no conoce?

Nada se oye.
En la casa vacía las preguntas—los pájaros—
se estrellan silenciosas contra el muro
y una muy tierna gota de sangre sustituye
a la huella del ala en el cemento.
Un instante fue el roce y destruidas
una a una se ocultan.

Dead Silence

Was I alone
going across time and the golden
gathering of fall; across tree
shadows on the hard,
restless water, and farther and farther out?

Was I—were we—talking in a fog
of pretend profiles
preening at my side: a pure-face,
night strange, with signs
of a remote language on its forehead and mouth?

Was I speaking to fog and shadow
or did anyone really hear me?

Did anyone hear?

The answer, was it a voice or the wind?
Was it a voice. Or the wild
water of that cruel and powerful river
unknown to love?

Dead silence.
In the empty house the questions—the birds—
crash soundless against the wall
and a tender drop of blood supplants
the trace of wing in cement.
An instant's graze, and one by one
they hide, ruined.

El silencio ¿no es mucho para cada criatura?
La eternidad es sólo un peligro invisible
porque las roncas voces de la montaña claman
por los cuerpos perdidos que hablaron a las sombras.

Nada se oye.
Pero entonces, ¿me oía?

El silencio es como una eternidad, sin fondo,
sin principio, una espalda
a la vida, a los hombres.

Para después no quiero contestación ninguna:
es aquí donde tuve la urgencia de saberlo.

Oh, sí, ya nada se oye.

Pero entonces ¿me oía?

> "The abandoned ruins of the dreams I left behind."
> *(De una canción popular inglesa.)*

Silence weighs a lot for every creature, doesn't it?
Eternity's only an invisible threat,
with mountain voices' hoarse crying
for lost bodies, for those who spoke with shadows.

Dead silence.
But then, did I hear myself?

Silence is like eternity, without end,
without beginning, a back turned
against life, against the human.

I don't want answers for afterward:
it's here and urgent where I needed to know.

Oh yes, dead silence now.

But then, did I hear myself?

"The abandoned ruins of the dreams I left behind."
(From a popular English song)

La última cena (Mujer de paja)

Recordar
no es volver a vivir. Sólo es mirar a otros,
los que fuimos
a través de una calle o tal vez cerca
del cielo. O en torno de una mesa.
No es torno: frente a frente
como los enemigos. O tan lejanos como
las aceras, las casas, los andenes,
las líneas férreas,
los árboles sin ramas
para abrazarse.

Fue una mesa tan sólo, Charlie, muy pequeña,
pero tan honda,
tan oscura dentro,
que yo desde mi orilla, él en la suya,
gritábamos inútiles palabras
—o silencios inútiles—
porque no oía yo y él no me oía.

Qué hermoso era el cristal
—las frescas cúpulas
del vino—y las candelas
tenues para el amor, para las manos
unidas por encima
del mantel, de los panes
exóticos salvados
de la voracidad por el dolor.

Nosotros, Charlie, dentro de la cúpula
flotando, como esferas, encerrados
entre palabras con envés, mordidas
como tristes monedas sin esfinge.

The Last Supper (Woman of Straw)

Remembering
is no return to life. It's only looking at other people,
who we once were,
across a street or maybe next to
heaven. Or around a table.
Not around: face to face
like enemies. Or as far away as
sidewalks, houses, platforms,
train tracks,
trees without branches
for embracing.

It was only a very small table, Charlie,
but so deep,
so dark inside,
that I from my far shore, he from his,
shouted useless words
—or useless silence—
because I wasn't listening to him and he wasn't listening to me.

How lovely the crystal was
—the fresh decanters
of wine—and the slender
candles for love, for hands
to be joined above
the tablecloth, above the exotic
breads rescued
from greed by grief.

We're inside the dome, Charlie,
floating, like spheres, enclosed
among words wrong side up, bitten
like sad, sphinxless coins.

No fueron sólo treinta
dineros. Era un largo
horizonte de cobres que no tintineaban
porque sólo más tarde pude saber que un cuerpo
fue vendido . . . (Qué cuerpo
me pregunto yo, Charlie.)

Recordar
no es volver a vivir.
No lo es en este caso: no se puede
ya volver a vivir sin otro cuerpo
—¿cuál?, sigo preguntando—
que fue vendido, que no está y no vuelve
porque no quedan ángeles de fuego
y no hace falta vigilar la tumba.

Mirando hacia detrás
la ciudad es un monstruo solitario
en el que el mar—mi mar—agita sus pañuelos
de adiós para los cuerpos subastados
cada día sin que ellos,
por supuesto, lo sepan.

Y en el sombrío corazón de acero,
sobre la mesa eternamente
vacía
(es un camino
de mesas con sus blancos
manteles empañados
de luna)
los dos vasos
con el hielo inocente reflejando
una ausencia infinita.

It wasn't just thirty
pieces. It was a long
horizon of coppers with no clinking
because only later I found out a body
was sold . . . (What body,
I ask myself, Charlie.)

Remembering
is no return to life.
Not in this case: you can't
return to life without another body
—which one?, I keep asking—
the one that was sold, that isn't here and won't return
because there are no more angels of fire
and no more need to guard the tomb.

Looking back,
the city is a solitary monster
where the sea—my sea—is waving its handkerchief
goodbye to the bodies auctioned off
every day without, of course,
the bodies knowing it.

And in the darkened steel heart,
over the table eternally
empty
(it's a long road
of tables, white
tablecloths moon-
misted),
two glasses
with ice innocently reflecting
an infinite absence.

Cita con una sombra

Para Joseph Therrien

> *"Qui es-tu," dit le Petit Prince. "Tu es bien joli."*
> *"Je suis un renard," dit le renard.*
> *"Viens jouer avec moi," lui proposa le Petit Prince. "Je suis tellement triste . . . "*
> *"Je ne puis pas jouer avec toi," dit le renard. "Je ne suis pas apprivoisé."*
> —Antoine de Saint-Exupéry

Yo no sé qué mensaje
tenía que decirte. Iba,
eso sí, hacia tu casa
cuando una voz me dijo:
Hay que pasar un cementerio
y a la derecha . . .

Por qué—me pregunté—*vive mi amigo*
en un lugar tan grave. Reflexioné:
Es triste
estar tan cerca de la muerte.

La casa estaba lejos
y crucé innumerables poblaciones dormidas,
cementerios de siglos perdidos en las sombras
del tiempo. No sentía
temor, pero su casa, ¿dónde?
¿Y para qué?

Appointment with a Shadow

For Joseph Therrien

> "Who are you," said the Little Prince. "You're very pretty."
> "I am a fox," said the fox.
> "Come and play with me," suggested the Little Prince. "I am so unhappy."
> "I can't play with you," said the fox. "I am not domesticated."
>   —Antoine de Saint-Exupéry

I don't know what message
I had to tell you. I was going,
naturally, toward your house
when a voice said to me:
*You will pass a cemetery
and on the right . . .*

Why—I asked myself—*does my friend live
in such a gloomy place.* And I thought:
*It's sad
to be so close to death.*

The house was far
and I crossed an uncountable, sleeping census,
cemeteries full of centuries lost in the shadows
of time. I wasn't
afraid, but his house, where was it?
And why?

Cirios y aguas. Piedras
con un temblor de soledad. Altivos
cuerpos de mármol desafiando el polvo
sobre altares de sombra.
Luego patios ancianos
con frescura estancada: en el recuerdo
aquel en que los pájaros dormían
sobre anchos abanicos.
                      ¿Están muertos
aquellos pájaros y aquella
vieja Universidad de vieja España
donde Ocnos tejía colores y perfumes
para el asno insaciable?

Yo buscaba la puerta
y nunca la encontraba.
Parecía alejarse en una huida inmóvil
o nadie respondía. ¿Cuántas
veces la misma y diferente puerta?

Manos me la indicaban, pero siempre
crucé otro cementerio. No aquel que conducía
a tu hogar de hombre vivo, alegre
tal vez.
      Las catedrales
que atravesé . . . Los altos mausoleos
de cardenales y de príncipes
y sus largas miradas
de helado fuego traspasando
la atmósfera de incienso. Hasta el menudo
barro de las doncellas, maltratado
en las Sibilas que cuidaban
el fuego—en el que ardían
los siglos—, me gritaba
su mensaje de polvo prematuro.

Cierges and fonts. Stones
with a tremor of solitude. Proud
marble bodies dueling the dust
over shadow altars.
Then ancient patios,
stagnant with freshness: in that memory
of birds dozing
on fleshy fans.
                Are those birds
dead, like that
old university, like Old Spain,
where Ocnos used to weave colors and scents
for an insatiable ass?

I kept looking for the door
and never found it.
It seemed to recede in immovable flight
or no one answered. How many
times was it the same yet a different door?

Hands pointed it out to me, but I
kept crossing cemeteries. Not the one that led
to your home, friend, alive and happy
maybe.
           The cathedrals
I went through ... the high mausoleums
of cardinals and princes
and their long looks
of frozen fire transfixed
in the perfumed air. Even the common
clay of maidens, mistreated
by Sibyls guarding
the fire—where centuries
burned—cried out a message of unripe dust.

Y allí entre las cenizas
las mudas plumas de una voz del aire.
Pensé: *el último día*
tendrá el niño de Ofelia un pájaro en la mano.

Tu puerta
estaba lejos. Parecía
alejarse, muy lenta, de mi puño
alzado y no podía
llamar.
      Amigo mío,
entre tú y mi visita,
cuántas muertes.

And there among the ashes
the mute plumes of a voice in the air.
I thought: *on the last day*
Ophelia's child will have a bird in his hand.

Your door
was far. It seemed
to recede, very slowly, from my raised
fist and I couldn't
knock.
        My friend,
between you and my visit,
so many deaths.

Metamorfosis

Se ha reducido su tamaño. Ahora
es más y más pequeña
y más oscura. Ahora es sólo
una sombrita en la pared,
allá en lo alto, donde están los nidos
desalquilados del invierno:
es sombra en la pared para el sol último.

Solía tener alas
y las vi alguna vez llegarse hasta una frente.
Su sonrisa
era como las otras y quedaba
también iluminando cuando ya era de noche:
tenía su manera de quedarse
cuando ya se había ido hacía mucho tiempo
por el reloj.

¿Qué ocurriría
para hacerse de pronto como el leve
residuo de una luz?

Nadie es culpable—dijo
la última vez—. *Alguien creerá que pudo*
—y dio su última sonrisa—: *era
mi viento personal que me esperaba
para soplar sobre la luz que quise
llegar a ser, y transformarme
en sombra, aquí en el muro,
para el último sol.*

Y después de un silencio: *Yo ya no necesito
estas alas antiguas.*

Metamorphosis

Her size has been reduced. Now
she is even smaller
and darker. Now she's only
a little shadow on the wall,
way up high, with the empty
nests of winter:
she's a shadow on the wall for the last sun.

She used to have wings.
Once I saw them spread about her.
Her smile
was like other smiles and even
shone at nightfall:
she had her way of staying
when the light had gone long ago
with the clock.

What could have happened
for her to suddenly become
like the filmy ash of light?

It's no one's fault—she said
the last time. *Someone thinks it was*
—and gave her last smile. *It was
the wind, my own, waiting
to blow out the light I wanted
to be, changing me
into shadow, here on the wall,
for the last sun.*

And after a silence: *Who needs
these old wings anyway.*

From: *Campanas en Sansueña*

Profundo mar azul

I.

Adivinando entre mi sueño el alba
del gato mal dormido, enfermo,
en el cuarto de abajo y de allá atrás,
mojado aunque no llueva,
y en esta tierra en la que nadie se me ha muerto,
oigo el dolor de la materia que se deshace,
de mis padres y madres lejanos,
que eran y no son, pero son y no se reconocen,
y quisiera pasar mi mano, humana todavía,
por su tristeza de ser que se transforma
en las cunas inmensas de los estratos.
A esa hora del alba en que adivino
al gato mal dormido, enfermo,
comprendo por qué sus manos detenidas
ya no se mueven y despejan la niebla;
por qué sus líneas se deshacen y no queda nada
que acariciar. En esa hora fría
en la que el día que viene es un teatro vacío
en el que los pasos resuenan.
Y para que todo comience más tarde
me doy media vuelta en la cama contando los años
en que alguien llevaba mi mano escribiendo la eme
con la a . . . : que su vida
sea una abeja de mármol
que en cien años no dirá nada a nadie.

From: *Bells in Sansueña*

Deep Blue Sea

I.

In my dream I divine the dawn
of the sick cat who slept badly,
in the backroom downstairs and beyond,
damp though it isn't raining,
and on this earth where nobody's died on me,
I hear the pain of matter disintegrating,
the pain of my mothers and fathers from long ago,
who once were and are not, but who, nevertheless, are and
 [can't recognize themselves,
and I'd like to pass my hand, still human,
over the sadness of their being, as it changes
into the immense cradle of the stratosphere.
At that hour of the dawn when I divine
the sick cat who slept badly,
I understand why their arrested hands
no longer move, dissolving the mist;
why their lines fall apart and nothing remains
for caressing. In that cold hour
when the day at hand is a vacant theater
of echoing footsteps.
So that everything can begin later,
I half turn in the bed, counting the years
when someone guided my hand writing an "m"
and an "a" together . . .: May your life
equal a marble bee
that in a hundred years means nothing to no one.

Dentro del teatro vacío
—a la hora del gato mal dormido en el cuarto de atrás—,
sé que empezaron a moverse
cuando los pies se les quedaron de cualquier manera
y cesaron de llorar para siempre. Pero no fueron muertos
sino profundamente dormidos
hasta que mi memoria llamó muerte a su sueño.
En ese instante
en que doy media vuelta en la cama,
y no voy a dormir pero tampoco a despertar,
porque son dolorosos los sueños
que se deshacen en olvido
dejando un rastro negro o humo
y muerte, un poco ya, temprano,
es cuando podría tomar posesión de la isla
sobre la que las cabezas dormidas no muestran
sino la dulce inclinación del cuello
reluciente en la luna.
A esa hora
podría regresar de las aguas de Donaghadee
o de la pálida bahía de Galway,
cruzando la niebla
de los borrachos que se han hecho dólmenes entre los dólmenes,
o los sueños de las niñas de mil novecientos
que en Halfpenny Bridge
muestran en su mirada los líquenes
de la locura más dulce. Porque bajo la noche
todos se mueven con la misma ternura
y la vieja Irlanda no es una bruja de matriz desecada
que se quita las pulgas sentada en la isla del Toro.

Inside the vacant theater
—just when the cat slept badly in the backroom—
I know they began to move about,
 their feet ended up any old way
and they stopped crying forever. But they weren't dead,
only deeply asleep
until my memory called their sleep death.
In that instant
if I half turn in the bed,
and I'm not going back to sleep, not going to wake up either,
it's because the dreams that dissolve in amnesia
are painful,
they leave a black smoky trace,
and now death, small and early,
is when I could take possession of the island,
above, sleeping heads reveal
only the sweet slope of the neck
glistening in the moonlight.
Then it is
I could return from the waters of Donaghadee
or from the pale Bay of Galway,
crossing the fog
of drunks turned into other dolmens among dolmens,
or the dreams of young girls of 1900
standing on Halfpenny Bridge
with their look of lichens
and the sweetest madness. Because in the night
they all move with the same tenderness
and old Ireland is no longer a witch with a dried womb
picking off fleas as she sits on John Bull's island.

Nada puede su diente sobre mi sueño
que se hace en otras sombras; nada sobre mis pasos
por la escena vacía
que cruza un gato del color de la gracia
y cientos de pájaros que van hacia el oeste
y regresan
y oleadas de hojas doradas—la ceniza
del verano—, o la boca,
en la que el tiempo olvidó la voz del niño,
que agita sus aspas irreparables en todos los vientos,
o mariposas que vienen a morir en las alfombras.

A veces pienso que no ha ocurrido
—no sé: ¿cómo ha ocurrido?—;
que en aquel *octubre lejano* no hubo días
y todo es un espacio único cruzado
por estrellas errantes, entre mil y mil siglos,
que siguen sucediéndose. Quito el hueco
de mi sombra en el aire: nada se hunde. ¿Estuve
alguna vez allí, entre ellos, sus manos,
sus amores, sus amplias
seguridades con pólizas? No quisiera
recordar, pero el tiempo
es sombra con cuchillo al volver una esquina.

She can't sink her teeth into my sleep,
made from other shadows; or into my footsteps
as they pass through the empty stage
where a cat the color of divine grace is crossing
and hundreds of birds going westward
and then returning
and waves of golden leaves—the ash
of summer— or the mouth,
in which time has forgotten the child's voice,
shaking bereft wings into the four winds,
or butterflies coming to die on the carpets.

Sometimes I think it hasn't happened
—I mean: how could it have happened?—
that in a *far-off October* days did not pass;
it's all a single space crossed by straggling stars,
and so on successively,
in saecula saeculorum. I take off the hollow dress
of my shadow in the air: nothing collapses. Was I
once there, among them, and their hands,
their loves, their ample
insurance policies? I'd rather not
remember, but time keeps turning the corner,
like a knife-wielding shadow.

II.

　　Yo tuve veinte años, pero no me di cuenta.
Y ahora no los recuerdo.
La luz que va creciendo en mí
dice
que no soy más que todo lo que gira
en ella;
no más que esta lechuga que está sobre la mesa,
nutrida con mis manos que ayudaron el ciclo
que los dioses protegen. Su verde perfección,
el secreto puño de aguas apretado
las olas tenues del corazón, o violentas,
que no puedo despegar sin ternura,
son el mensaje de una tragedia que nadie representa y yo veo
pensando en que esta noche he dado media vuelta en la cama
porque este cuerpo empieza a molestarme
como un abrigo estrecho
que hay que quitarse para estar más cómoda.

II.

    I was once twenty, but didn't know I was.
And now I don't remember.
The light growing in me
says
that I am nothing more than things spinning
in it;
nothing more than this lettuce on the table,
nourished by my hands helping the cycle
that the gods protect. Its green perfection,
the secret, tightened fist of water,
the barely visible, violent waves of the heart,
that I can't pull off without tenderness,
are a tragic message no one recites and I see,
thinking, tonight, I half turned in the bed
because this body is beginning to bother me
like a tight-fitting coat
you have to take off to be more comfortable.

III.

    Yo tuve veinte años, pero no lo sabía.
Y ahora no los recuerdo,
aunque quisiera tenerlos aquí, en mi mano,
exentos ya de mí,
como se tienen una llave o un libro
y se miran.
Quisiera ver, a un tiempo, su luz y su sombra,
y no sólo su ausencia; no sólo
su ignorancia de la muerte;
no sus fragmentos perdidos;
no su introito a las sombras.
    Pero están solos vagando al otro lado del muro,
girando en un viento incesante,
en la extensa memoria en que primero habló el odio
revestido, como siempre, de la cándida ropa del amor
                                       [traicionado.

Y ante las dos esfinges,
el punto de partida y el deseo
de no volver a vivirlos—jamás, jamás, jamás—,
pero de recordarlos
como podría recordarse una mano amputada
que fue hermosa y que quizá fue hermosa,
¿hacia dónde dirigir la mirada?

III.

    I was once twenty, but didn't know I was.
And now I don't remember the years,
though I'd like to have them here, in my hand,
set apart from me,
the way you hold a key or a book,
the way you look at them.
I'd like to see their light and shadow together,
and not simply their absence; not simply
their ignorance of death
or their lost fragments,
their introit to the shades.
    But they are alone wandering toward the other side of
                                                          [the wall,
twisting in a restless wind,
in long memory when hate first spoke
dressed, as always, in the simple clothing of love betrayed.

But before the two sphinxes,
before the point of origin and the desire
to not relive them—never, never, never—
but to remember them
like you might remember an amputated hand
that was once beautiful, or perhaps was beautiful,
where to set the gaze?

IV.

    Nunca el origen
perdido en la llanura donde primero fue el odio.
Nunca más el paisaje salado y polvoriento
donde puedo encontrar mi imagen sentada en una piedra
—sombra que fue otras sombras—
contemplando todavía las dos esfinges
—la del amor vestido de odio;
la del odio vestido con la cándida ropa del amor traicionado—,
tratando, todavía, de reconocer la luz
tras de las viejas máscaras cambiantes.
Porque si pongo mi pie en la orilla del uno de noviembre
hoy, mañana y ayer serán, en aire, polvo.

IV.

    Never again lost origins
on the plain where hate first existed.
Never again the salt- and dust-filled landscape
where I find my image resting on a stone
—a shadow of other shadows—
still seeing the two sphinxes
—one is love dressed in hate;
the other is hate dressed in the simple clothing of
                                           [betrayed love—
still trying to recognize the light
behind ancient, shifting masks.
Because if I step onto the shore of the first of November
today, tomorrow and yesterday will be dust in the air.

Grupo de hombres (Faculty Meeting)

Una manga de pavo real que golpea una espalda.
Curva solitaria bajo pipa reticente, soñadora,
humeante de frío, soledad.
Un perfil,
un hombre que es sólo su perfil
cabalgado por nieves prematuras.
Unas manos que han olvidado riendas
en Montana y enjugado
sudor y cuero
—yacen, cuando esto escribo de recuerdo,
dentro de un monte
de solitarias aves visitado—;
cuando las vi, caían,
y eran todo su hombre.
Un belfo
discretamente nazi
emite un gorgoparloteo que se posa en los tímpanos,
abriéndose camino por la selva de los enormes cráneos.
                                                               Y unos ojos,
un hombre que es sólo sus ojos,
mira al que es sólo su perfil,
al que es sólo una pipa,
al que es sólo su gorgoteo
y al que es sólo una manga de pavo.
Y lo ve todo lógico.

Group of Men (Faculty Meeting)

A peacock's tail hitting a back.
Solitary curve beneath a reticent, dreaming pipe,
puffing at cold and loneliness.
A profile.
A man who is only his profile
capped by premature snows.
Hands that have forgotten Montana
reins and dried
sweat and leather
—lie, as I write this from memory,
under a mountain
visited by solitary birds.
When I saw them, they were falling,
they were the man himself.
A thick lower lip
discreetly nazi
emits a twittering gurgle that perches on
                         [our eardrums,
opening up a road through the forest of swelling skulls.
                                        And eyes,
a man who is only his eyes,
looks at the man who is only his profile,
at the man who is only a pipe,
at the man who is only his gurgle
at the man who is only a peacock's tail.
And it all seems perfectly logical to him.

(Sobre el hombre que es sólo sus manos
silencio: siempre tienen razón los que mueren).
No han oído
el latir del reloj. Nadie ha visto
que una luz se ha encendido allá fuera.   No huelen
que ha empezado a llover.   Y alguien llega.
Cada uno en su escorzo
cortésmente se roen, cristalinos
ratones, doctorados en polvo y musarañas.
                    Huyamos.
Si supieran
que sólo son los huesos
del amor, cáscaras de una fe, basura
de los niños que fueron y pellejo
de aquellos que esperaron
que fuesen, romperían
las lunas, matarían
las llamas
y saldrían al mundo
a embadurnarnos con su buena nueva.

(Hanging over the man who is only his hands:
   silence: those who die are always right.)
      They haven't heard
the tick of the clock. No one's noticed
that a light has clicked on out there. They don't smell
the start of rain. Then someone arrives.
Each man tight in his skin,
politely they gnaw one another, crystalline
bookworms with doctorates in dust and vermin.
                  Let's beat it.
If they just knew
they're only the bones
of love, the shell of faith, the debris
of the children they were and the skin
of what they hoped
to be, they'd shatter
the moonlight, knock off
the flames
and bust out,
ready to preach the good news.

El tiempo me recuerda

Recordar no es siempre regresar a lo que ha sido.
En la memoria hay algas que arrastran extrañas maravillas;
objetos que no nos pertenecen o que nunca flotaron.
La luz que recorre los abismos
ilumina años anteriores a mí, que no he vivido
pero recuerdo como ocurrido ayer.
Hacia mil novecientos
paseé por un parque que está en París—estaba—
envuelto por la bruma.
Mi traje tenía el mismo color de la niebla.
La luz era la misma de hoy
—setenta años después—
cuando la breve tormenta ha pasado
y a través de los cristales veo pasar la gente,
desde esta ventana tan cerca de las nubes.
En mis ojos parece llover
un tiempo que no es mío.

Time Remembers Me

Remembering doesn't always mean a return to what was.
In memory algae cling to strange, wondrous sights:
objects that don't belong to us or never floated.
The light ranging through chasms
turns the beam on years before I existed, that I haven't lived
but I remember as if it were yesterday.
Around 1900
I strolled through a park enveloped in fog
that is in Paris—or used to be.
My dress was the color of mist.
The light was the same as today
—seventy years later—
when a summer storm is over
and through the panes I see the people passing,
from this window so close to the clouds.
In my eyes a time that is not mine
seems to be dropping rain.

España, eres un largo invierno

"España es un largo invierno".
—Thomas Merton

El invierno va a quedarse vacío.
Dientes de hielo—flor árbol asesinados—
huecos con ecos resumiendo
en vacío el frío interminable. Blanca
y no cándida la nieve distribuye
la muerte donde antes
la llama ardió, el deseo
o la fe poderosa—con un gusano dentro—.
    Los ojos minerales de la fiera—enigma o toro—petrifican
el clamor de las lanzas, invernales
espíritus, que yacen—moscas mierda
de perros—en rincones
señalados por una cruz de palo
—con su gusano dentro—.   Bizqueando,
tarareando—con su gusano dentro—, España pasa y duerme
—funda de hielo para el alma; cuarto
habitado de polvo y musarañas—
muerta aquella alta frente
que enloqueció de tanto estar despierta; mudo el labio,
yacente el dedo, en remolinos
de barro y nieve oculto el pensamiento; rotos
los ritmos de los gestos, muecas mudas,
bobosdecoria destilando jugo
bendito, chupadedos, manosdiestras
en el mojar el pan en sangre hermana.

Spain is a Long Winter

> "Spain is a long winter."
> —Thomas Merton

Winter is going to remain vacant.
Teeth of ice—flower tree assassinated—
recessed echoes containing
in a vacuum the unending cold. White
and guilty, the snow distributes
death where before
the flame burnt, desire
or powerful faith—with a worm inside.
   The wild beast's mineral eyes—an enigma or bull—
                              [turn to stone
the clamoring of lances, winter
spirits, that lie—flies dog
shit—in corners
marked by a wooden cross
—with its worm inside.
                        Squinting,
humming—with its worm inside—Spain endures and sleeps
—an icy cover for the soul; a room
dusted in vermin—
the high forehead's dead
that went crazy being awake so much; the lips are mute,
the finger still, thought hidden
in swirls of mud and snow; the ragged
rhythms of gestures, gaping grimaces,
simplesimons distilling the blessed
fluid, fingerlickers, jacksprats
for the dipping of bread in human blood.

Inútil preguntarse: apaguemos las luces.
Esto es sólo un invierno con su gusano. Habría
que gritar a la frente de los siglos: "Hombre,
si vienes a esta tierra, da la vuelta, desnace;
que no te pesquen en la nada y traigan
a este lugar, cogido de una oreja.
         En esta eterna nieve
las flores mueren y los dioses ríen".
Nunca España—su sueño—:
sólo un gordo gusano devorante.

It's useless to ask: just put out the lights.
This is only one winter with its worm. You'd have to
face the centuries screaming: "Look, man,
if you come to this country, go back, abort,
so they don't fish you out of the void and bring you
to this place, dragged by the ears.
                                        In this eternal snow
flowers die and gods laugh."
Never Spain—her sleep—
only a fat devouring worm.

Eso

Eso, a lo que han gritado ¡fuera! hace mucho tiempo,
eso, eso que está ahí, en la orilla,
¿por qué se obstina aún
en subir
desde la noche a la luz que no le pertenece?
¿Por qué se agarra
a la rama azul de la esperanza y vive y vive
y no sabe otra cosa
más que vivir?
             ¿Qué es eso,
de qué materia,
que flota todavía, que trepa,
que respira y casi
sonríe y se recuesta
en el color de la amapola?
   Quién ha traído eso
y lo ha dejado ahí, entre nosotros, si no sabe
más que vivir,
más que esperar acaso
y no aprende su nada: su ser único.
Si mucho antes de ser
no era. Todo lo que eso vive
ha sido ya vivido, hace edades.
                      Y sabiéndolo, sigue.
¿Está esperando un poco de calor?
¿Acaso que alguien diga: "Sí, te conocemos"?
¿O tal vez otra cosa que ni sabe?
   ¿Por qué no se ha dejado caer sobre las aguas
y olvidar?

That Thing

That thing they screamed at a long time ago: get out!
That, that thing there, on the border,
why does it persist, still,
in moving up
from the darkness to the light that doesn't belong to it?
Why does it cling
to the blue branch, hope, and live and live
and doesn't know anything
except to live?   What is that thing,
what's it made of,
that it still floats, climbs,
breathes and nearly
smiles and leans
into the color of the poppy?
   Who brought that thing
and left it there, among us, when it only
knows life,
knows hope, perhaps,
and doesn't see it's nothingness: that it's only being.
Long before being after all,
it wasn't. Everything that it lives
has already been lived, ages ago.
                        And knowing that,
                            [it goes on.
Is it waiting for a little warmth?
That someone should say maybe: "Yes, we know you"?
Or perhaps something else it doesn't even know?
   Why doesn't it just fall down dead into the water
and forget?

Si una mariposa se detiene en tu mano, mátala

                        Nadie sabía quién era.
Tenía mil colores en las alas
que se llevaba el viento dos, tres veces al día.
Cantaba cosas locas
cosas llenas de gotas de agua que luego resbalaban por las
                    [hojas hacia la tierra y hacia el mar.
Y a veces florecía en invierno, equivocada,
y se echaba a reír y se iba junto al fuego a secarse los pétalos
                              [mojados de tormenta.
      Nadie sabía quién era . . .
Un verano fue nieve y navidad y llamaba a las puertas,
                        [tiritando. Le mostraban
calendarios, relojes, documentos. Y se sentó a morir de frío
                    [aquel agosto. En sus ojos hallaron
los estanques helados, los pájaros dormidos, los caminos
                                    [desiertos.

If a Butterfly Lights on Your Hand, Kill It

                                        No one knew who it was.
It had a thousand colors on wings
the wind would carry two, three times a day.
It used to sing crazy things,
things that were heavy with drops of water and trickled
        [down leaves toward the earth, toward the sea.
And sometimes it would bloom in winter, by mistake,
took to laughing and sitting next to the fire to dry petals
                            [wet from a storm.
    No one knew who it was . . .
One summer there was snow and Christmas and it called
at all the doors, trembling. They showed it
calendars, watches, documents. And it sat down to die
        [of the cold that August. In its eyes they found
frozen ponds, sleeping birds, deserted roads.

El rostro vuelto hacia la pared

Todo el mundo conoce la ancha gota
que va de noche en noche, de almohada
en almohada, de mejilla en mejilla,
pero nadie la llama por su nombre.
　No tiene nombre.
Es tú y es yo. Será y fue todos. Cae
como una lava transparente y fría
del ojo mar espina estupefacta.
　No tiene nombre.
Sale cuando las sombras. Cuando todo
se queda al otro lado de la puerta
dejándonos
entre cuatro paredes y un espejo
—donde es mejor no verse—.
　Otras veces no cae:
hierve en el fondo de los cuerpos,
encharca las gargantas, desintegra
las rocas, sale, escapa
por debajo de puertas.
Pero nunca se ha ido: sólo es que no la vemos.
Prosigue su trabajo:
hormiguear por el trigal triunfante,
preparando los vasos—laboriosa—
hasta el bronco estallido.
　No tiene nombre. Y de día olvidamos
el viaje difícil de la noche
por esa inmensa agua. Y elegimos los cómplices,
las sonrisas, los templos,
el fragor, el abrigo
del honrado trabajo.

The Face Turned to the Wall

Everyone sees the ample drop of water
that goes from night to night, from pillow
to pillow, from cheek to cheek,
but no one calls it by name.
    It has no name.
It's you and me. It will be and was everyone. It falls
like cold, transparent lava
from the eyes sea the startled spine.
    It has no name.
It comes out with the shadows. When everything
remains on the other side of the door
leaving us
between four walls and a mirror
—where it's better not to look.
    Other times it doesn't fall:
it boils in the bellies of bodies,
clogs throats, pulverizes
stones, gets out, escapes
underneath doors.
But it never goes away: we just don't see it.
Its work goes on:
weeviling through flushed fields of wheat,
preparing crystal laboriously
until there is the harsh shatter.
    It has no name. And by day we forget
the arduous journey of night
through that immense water. And we choose accomplices,
smiles, churches,
the clatter and cloak
of honest work.

Nos escondemos
de ella. Pero viene
cada noche y
cada día y
todas las semanas y
todos los relojes, eras, extensiones
de edades que ya nadie
puede nombrar.
No tiene nombre.
Es agua y no es agua.

    Estaba aquí desde el principio.
Y se parece a la sed. Del agua tiene
la inmensidad,
la apariencia de lecho que nos lleva;
el que diluye los colores
y el sabor de lo dulce y de lo amargo;
el que no podamos entender su lenguaje
ni su va y viene acompasado
en un orden, si justo, muy amargo.
    Tiene nombre. Pero nadie lo sabe.
Cuando las luces se van apagando
y el último sonido se esparce y desaparece,
cuando borramos el fulgor de la estrella
con nuestro párpado
para el que el sueño es una vieja rutina,
ella desciende
e ilumina un paisaje secreto
que al llegar el día olvidamos.
Pero nos queda el recuerdo
de que antes del sueño profundo
hemos llorado

We hide
from it. But it comes
every night and
every day and
every week and
every watch, era, rock
of ages that now no one
can name.
It has no name.
It's water and it isn't water.

    It was here from the beginning.
And it's like thirst. It has
the immensity of water,
the appearance of a bed carrying us away;
the fact that it thins colors
and the taste of sweet and bitter;
the fact that we can't understand its language
or its regular comings and goings
within an order that is just, but hard to swallow.
    It has a name. But no one knows it.
When lights are going out
and the last sound scatters and disappears,
and we rub out the radiance of stars
with our eyelids
for whom our sleep is an old routine,
it descends
and lights up a secret landscape
forgotten when day comes.
But memory remains:
before deep sleep
we cried

por nuestras manos y por todas las manos,
por nuestros ojos y por todos los ojos,
por nuestra niñez y por todos los niños,
por nuestra muerte y por todas las muertes,
por nuestra vislumbre y por todas las adivinaciones,
por nuestra complicidad con el día y por todos los cómplices,
por nuestro temor y por todos los temores,
por haber sido defraudados y por todos los fraudes,
por nuestra esperanza y por todos los templos,
por nuestros crímenes y por todos los verdugos,
por nuestra raza efímera y por todos los mundos a la deriva,
por las tiernas hojas de los árboles que aún no han florecido y
[por toda la belleza
que la esperanza hizo forma.
Porque no hemos aprendido a ser arrastrados en silencio
por ese agua que de la vida no mana
ni conduce a la vida ni a su nombre y lloramos
por lo que no lloran ni la hoja ni el pájaro,
ni el ciervo herido ni los peces mudos.

for our hands, for all the hands,
for our eyes, for all the eyes,
for our childhood, for all the children,
for our death, for all the deaths,
for our intuition, for all the flashes of insight,
for our complicity with the day, for all accomplices,
for our terror, for all terrors,
for our deception, for all deceits,
for our hope, for all the churches,
for our crimes, for all the executioners,
for our ephemeral race, for all the worlds a-drift,
for the tender leaves of trees yet to bloom and for all
                                                [the beauty
that hope gave shape.
Because we haven't learned to be dragged in silence
by water that doesn't flow from life
or lead to life or to its name, because we weep
for what neither leaf nor bird
nor wounded deer nor soundless fish weeps.

Nota al pie de una historia

Variación a las Bachianas Brasileñas núm. 5 de Villa-Lobos

Ha comenzado el último
adiós. Van a decirse
las fórmulas del fin. He de dejarlo
todo cuando oiga: "Consumatum
est". Comprendo ahora
y por fin la alegría
de estar entre vosotras, sombras ásperas,
seres que me cruzáis
en ciudades, de noche.
Arboles, rocas, rosas, comprendo la alegría
de que estéis junto a mí con vuestra equívoca
presencia que, de niña,
no pude comprender y con vosotros
jugaba. No sois para jugar: para decirme
adiós y regresar en otras primaveras
del mundo recordándome
tal vez, a vuestro modo. (Ser un día
recuerdo de una roca; memoria
de una rosa en un jardín
en la luna habitada, es ser).

Footnote to History

Variation on the Brazilian Bachianas no. 5 by Villa-Lobos

The last goodbye has
begun. They're going to say
the formulas of the finish. And I will have
to leave it all when I hear: "Consumatum
est." I understand now,
finally, the joy
of being among you, harsh shadows,
beings who pass by me
in cities, at night.
Trees, rocks, roses, I understand the joy
of your being next to me with your elusive
presence that, as a child,
I could not understand when I played
with you. You aren't meant for playing: but for telling me
goodbye and returning again in the spring
of the world to remember me
perhaps, in your own way. (To be one day
the memory of a stone; the memory
of a garden rose
on a populated moon, that is being.)

Creí que había venido para siempre
y estaba
triste. Ahora he descubierto
la muerte por las simas
y la vida en las crestas
de la piel. Ahora es todo
distinto: me preparo
con desgana a partir y estoy más cerca
de los que aún no saben y los que están marchando.
    Mi identidad
no me la dio el amor sino la muerte
—amor es una sombra tras las claras ventanas,
el grito de una hora
que muere,
un portazo violento—,
y gozo del espacio, de la luz, de los aires
de cristal, de los largos
silencios, de los ríos
que pasan:
de toda la hermosura que ahora es mía y que vivo.
La catedral de sombra tiene luz todavía.

     I thought I had arrived forever
and I was
sad. Now I have discovered
death in the cracks
and life in the tufts
of skin. Now everything is
different: I prepare myself
halfheartedly to depart and I am nearer
to those who still don't know, to those who are traveling.
     My identity
isn't a gift of love, but of death
—love is a shadow behind clear windows,
the cry of an hour
that dies,
a violent bang of the door—
I bathe in space, light, crystal
air, long
silences, passing
rivers:
all the beauty that is mine now, to live.
The cathedral of shadows still sheds light.

Mi positivo es una estrella

No sé de dónde vino
ni qué era aquella gota de luz sobre mi frente.
Perseveró sumisa, conduciéndome
—porque yo sueño con estrellas
que me traducen el misterio
cuando los ejes están a punto de romperse—.
                    Días y días.
Sobre mi frente, sin tocarla. Mientras
las muchedumbres me tragaban,
sin verla
tan dulcemente detenida,
sostenida en el aire. Luego se fue
dejándome
fuera de un alto y silencioso muro carcelario;
fuera de las cancelas y de las puertas mudas. *Fuera.*
        Después sentí caer mi cuerpo, sin ruido,
hacia un fondo de fieras,
aprisionado entre dos altas
paredes: ciega una, como el suelo de un horno.
La otra, de cristal: tras ella el mundo
y la luz de los seres.
                    Sin angustia
descendía mi cuerpo—las manos resbalando
por la pared más densa, por la puerta
cerrada eternamente y tras de ella
adiviné los huesos que me dieran, con la vida, la muerte.
                            [Me detuve sin miedo
—tal vez la estrella en mí pensaba—y me volví, despacio
para mirar por el cristal. No me veía
la escena familiar: bajo la luz dorada del futuro
mi hermano—lentos ojos, nieve
en el cabello—jugaba con sus nietos en torno de una mesa.

My Absolute is a Star

I don't know where it came from
or what that drop of light on my face was.
It held on, humbly, leading me
—because I dream of translating
stars to show me the mystery
when the core's about to melt.
                Days and days.
On my face, not touching it. While
crowds were swallowing me up,
not seeing it
so sweetly stopped,
sustained in the air. Then it went away
leaving me
outside the high and silent prison wall;
outside mute doors and gates. *Outside*.
    Later I felt my body drop, soundless,
toward the belly of beasts,
imprisoned between two high
walls: one was pitch black, like the bottom of an oven.
The other, clear glass: and behind it, the world
and the light of being.
                My body kept descending
without torment—hands sliding
past the thickest wall, past the eternally
closed door and behind it
I guessed what bones they'd given me, with life, death.
                                [I stopped unafraid
—maybe the star in me was thinking—and turned slowly
to look through the glass. The scene
wasn't familiar to me: under a golden future light
my brother—slow eyes, snow
in his hair—played with his grandchildren around a table.

Adiviné mi ausencia en el silencio
y hasta el olvido de mi ausencia. Crucé el cristal
—viví un instante del futuro—, toqué su brazo, dije:
"Estoy aquí", como en los días
de mis largos viajes. Pero mi voz llegaba
del otro lado del silencio: no oyeron.
Y me encontré de nuevo
en las nieves calladas del otro continente.

I saw my absence in the silence
and even my absence forgotten. Passing through the crystal,
—to live an instant of the future— and touching his arm,
                                        [I said:
"I'm back," like in the days
when I traveled a lot. But my voice arrived
from the other side of silence: they didn't hear me.
And I found myself once more
in the silent snow of another continent.

From: *Viejas voces secretas de la noche*

Viejas voces secretas de la noche

I.

    A un árbol doble llamo soy. Hacia opuestos caminos
sus troncos van. Y la raíz no sabe
a cuál de ellos nutrir, amar, reconocer.
Arduo fue para uno de ellos—el que mira a poniente—,
caminar sobre horas derrocadas
que tuvieron su egregio momento, de voces
sin sonido—boca
como pez que se ahoga en nuestro aire—,
de cabellos que huían
dejando a un lado la fuente que sonríe,
a otro la fuente que lloraba,
no bebiendo en ninguna, cruzando
sobre cuatro ríos, sobre cuatro puentes.

    Sobre cuatro puentes,
con la muerte y la vida a la izquierda
—ancho mar cambiante—,
la otra rama va.
              No llega.
                        Siempre isla
sin vocación
—entre cuatro ríos, entre cuatro puentes—,
            ni ancla, la raíz
no tiene ganas de levantar el pañuelo:
está mojado y cae. Carece de papel,
lápiz, botella que navegue a otras manos:
juega con sus mengues
mientras su rato de isla transcurre.

From: *Ancient Secret Voices of the Night*

Ancient Secret Voices of the Night

I.

A twinned tree I call being. The trunks point
to opposite roads. And the roots don't know
which of them to nourish, to love, to recognize.
For one of them—the one pointing west—it was painful
to walk over squandered hours
that once had their shining moment, voices
without sound—the mouth
like a fish drowning in our air—
hair flying
leaving to one side the smiling fountain,
to the other the crying fountain,
drinking in neither, crossing
over four rivers and four bridges.

    Over four bridges,
with death and life to the left
—a wide mutable sea—
goes the other branch.
                      It doesn't arrive.
                                    Always an island
without a calling
—between four rivers and four bridges—
                        unanchored, the root
has no desire to lift the handkerchief:
it's wet and falls. Lacking paper,
pencil, or a bottle to sail to other hands,
it plays the devil's game
while its turn as an island lapses.

Inútil enviar mensajero—que almendro pudo ser—
a reunir las piezas del mapa de las sombras;
a que por mí averigüe dónde
dejar doblados los recuerdos; qué imagen
grabar en las memorias fugitivas.
                              Viejas voces
¿lo dirán en mi oído?
Han borrado el camino hacia las cunas
y le llamamos muerte a los regresos.

¡Cómo nos han confundido los hombres,
el zumbido lento de sus cerebros!
Trabajar en sus mentes
es oficio engañoso. Sus ciencias y artimañas
expolian la materia de su entraña sagrada:
la hacen útil, mortal y transitoria.
Cuando los siento reinar sobre el mundo
y gobernarlo pisando las hormigas,
atropellando a los perros,
sin detenerse a mirar a una gallina coja
ni parir a una gata—con su hondo
desconsuelo de gata, madre
como cualquiera otra madre de ellos—;
cuando los veo tocar, palpar,
codiciosos,
lo que otros, con trabajo, extrajeron del huevo
                              de la tierra,
echando en sus espaldas temporales la labor de los siglos,
y sólo es, para ellos, cosa, bulto
que usan, que se comen, que merecen,
se me extraña que ardiera aquella mariposa
ni que ahora sus cenizas giren entre las ramas.
    Mas debo, entre los días, esforzarme
en que las noches me parezcan noches
como antes, como siempre, como a todos.

Useless to send a messenger—likely the almond tree—
to fit the pieces into the shadow map;
suppose you could find out through me
where to leave folded relics; what image
to engrave in fugitive memories.
   Ancient voices,
will they whisper it in my ear?
They've effaced the tracks to the cradles
where we call the return trip death.

   How men have confused us,
with the slow buzzing of their brains!
Working inside their minds
is a deceitful profession. Their science and strategems
plunder matter from its sacred site:
make it useful, mortal and transitory.
When I see them lord it over the world
and govern by stepping on ants,
running over dogs,
without stopping to look at a lame hen
or a cat giving birth—with her deep
feline distress, a mother
like any other mother, like theirs—
when I see them touch, feel up,
greedily,
what others painfully extracted from the womb of the earth,
heaving onto their temporary shoulders the labor of centuries,
and it's only, for them, a thing, a shape
they use, eat up, or win,
I am not shocked that a butterfly should burn,
that its ashes now drift among the branches.
   But I must, these days, force myself
to make nights seem like nights to me
like before, like always, like everyone else.

II.

    La noche es ahora oscuridad
y caminar por los cuartos que ilumina la luna.
                                        No temer
las lentas sombras de los árboles
sobre bultos de muebles apagados;
oír, tratar de oír, de sorprender, mejor, las voces
que parecen de fuera y son de dentro.
La noche es andar y andar, conjurando, tejiendo
—no para darles vida, sino digno reposo—,
todo lo que olvidé olvidándolo. Memoria:
el espejo infinito sin azogue.
¿Cómo se han apagado tantas luces eternas?
"Eternas", yo decía. Sí, eternas.
Pero apagadas. Lumbres apagadas.
La noche es caminar
buscando ángulos de luz.
Caminar, escuchar, esperar . . . Lo sorprendente
es que la historia es vieja.

III.

    Ya no sé si la noche
lo es también para mí, como tampoco
sé quién me dice: "dilo".
Y lo digo—escribo—y ahí está: mirándome en sus letras;
dejándose mirar y que pregunte: "¿qué quiere decir esto?"

II.

    The night is darkness now
and walking through rooms lit by the moon.
                             Not fearing
the slow shades of trees
over the forms of dimmed furniture;
hearing, or trying to hear, to surprise I mean, the voices
that seem to come from outside and are from inside.
Night is a walking, a walking, conjuring, weaving
—not to give them life, but a worthy rest—
everything I forgot, by forgetting it. Memory:
mirror: infinity minus quicksilver.
How have so many eternal lights gone out?
"Eternal," I said. Yes, eternal.
But gone out. Lights gone out.
Night is a walking
looking for angles of light.
Walking, listening, waiting . . . The surprising thing:
is it's an old story.

III.

    I don't know anymore if the night
is night for me also, like I don't know
who says to me: "say it."
And I say it—I write—and there it is: looking at me
                                    [with its letters;
letting me look at it and ask: "What does this mean?"

Siento como una presencia en la oscuridad.
Una presencia que no toco aunque mis dedos
casi la rozan. No como a una seda
sino como a un amarillo profundo
sobre el que un rey y una reina se amasen.
Y hay un río—me lo dice la noche—,
que corrió sobre piedras
y lavó sangres y armaduras, bocas de caballos
sedientos; un río de amor
cuyo sonido me llega de muy lejos
y al que no quiero regresar. Pero corre
por mi apagado corazón, como la voz que dice:
> *En la sala está la dama*
> *namorando su cojín . . .*

Mas la dama se va por un camino de rosales en sombra
—se oyen surtidores, cruzan aromas, murmuran dueñas—
y bajo la luz de hoy recojo del pasado
un almadraque, con unicornio en su raso podrido,
sobre el que un rey y una reina se amaron.

I feel something like a presence in the dark.
A presence I can't touch though my fingers
almost brush it. Not like silk
but like deep yellow
and on top a king and a queen loving each other.
And there's a river—the night tells me this—
that ran over stones
and washed blood and armor, the mouths
of thirsty horses; a river of love
whose sound reaches me from far away
and to which I do not wish to return. But it runs
through my muted heart, like the voice that says:
         *in her chamber is the lady
         caressing a cushion . . .*
But the lady departs in a bower of shaded roses
—fountains spurt, aromas drift, duennas murmur—
and under this day's light I take from the past
a pillow, with a unicorn on rotted satin,
and on top a king and a queen loved each other.

IV.

    Silencio, negra puerta que me excedes,
como un halo que arrastro o que me lleva;
enorme puerta sin una mano de oro
para llamar y que alguien oiga y abra.
Te veo. No te ve nadie más que yo. Te palpo.
Pongo mi oído sobre ti: la noche
es lo que oigo. Y no comprendo
por qué esta puerta que en mi cuerpo crece.

    (Una puerta que es mucho mayor que mi cuerpo.
Una puerta que desborda mi contorno).

    No llamo a esa puerta, no la araño, no grito.
Espero.
Llamaría, la arañaría, gritaría
porque va a amanecer y quiero oír
las voces que murmuran tras la puerta,
tras la piedra. Sí, tras esa sombra, es cierto.
Una puerta en forma de sombra.
Una pregunta en forma de puerta.
Una pregunta ensombrecida de distancia.

IV.

    Silence, a black door overrunning me,
like a halo that I'm dragging or that's dragging me;
an enormous door without a golden hand
to knock upon so that someone hears and opens.
I see you. Only I, no one else, see you. I touch you.
I place my ear over you: the night
is what I hear. And I don't understand
why this door is growing inside my body.

(A door that is much larger than my body.
A door that overflows my shape.)

    I don't knock at this door, or scratch it, or shout.
I wait.
I would knock, scratch it, shout
because the sun's rising and I want to hear
the voices murmuring behind the door,
behind the stone. Yes, even behind that shadow.
A door in the form of a shadow.
A question in the form of a door.
A question darkened with distance.

Orden del sueño

    Cuando entré a despedirme de los ámbitos
a los que ya rendí mi adiós, mas no mi olvido,
la amada sombra estaba recortándose,
cual negativo de una antigua foto,
sobre lechosa luz de día que declina:
oscura luz o sombra iluminada,
símbolo, pudo ser, de una terrible
desdicha.
    Mi sorprendida mano,
que hallarse sola se creía,
puso luz en la estancia, no en la sombra,
ni en el enigma que el tiempo me acercaba
para borrar, con cada beso sabio,
un dolor.
    Ya pasados, recordarlos no puedo.
Se me fueron sus nombres y ocasiones.
Sólo hablan en mí sus voces confundidas.
Y ni eso, a veces: un viento que se aleja
entre golpes de mar, nieve que cae.
    A través de los sueños
se abre paso el olvido, y los rencores
decaen, lentamente, como otoño ante invierno.
La noche y sus preciosas criaturas
limpias de su pasado miserable;
salvadas de ellas mismas, de mí misma,
de pie sobre otra tierra: un paraíso.

The Order of Dream

    When I went in to say goodbye to the places marked,
to take leave again, yet not to forget,
shadow, dearly loved, had cut a silhouette,
like the negative of an old photo,
over the milky light of the declining day:
dark light or blazing shadow,
a symbol, perhaps, of some terrible
sorrow.   My hand, surprised,
thinking itself alone,
left light in the room, not in the shadow,
not in the mystery time brought near
to erase, with each wise kiss,
pain.   Gone forever, I can't remember them.
Names and dates have left me.
Only blurred voices speak in me.
Sometimes not even that: a wind retreating
in the surging sea, in falling snow.
                        Passing through dreams
amnesia marks the path, and hatred
fades slowly, like autumn before winter.
Night, its rare creatures,
free of their miserable past;
saved from themselves, from me,
stand on another earth: a paradise.

Poemas limítrofes

I.

El vacío no es una silla
frente al desierto: es el silencio
del alma. Es un corazón
sin luz. Es ver esta mano
 —llegada desde una mano más pequeña
 y perdida, tal vez muy dulce—,
quieta, pero no muerta: siendo lo que muere,
ceniza de lo que fue. Cambiando. Moviéndose
en su profunda inmovilidad
 —así se mueve . . . el tiempo—.
Haciéndose presente sobre la mesa.
Ajena y viva. Un objeto exento
que fue una mano y ahora es otra mano
que no deja su huella en la piedra
sino en la arena: agua
del gran desierto aquél.
 O una mano
que es una silla vacía frente al mismo desierto
 —sabré qué digo ahora
 dentro de algunos años—.
 Una mano
que cuelga de un brazo que pertenece a un hombro
y este hombro a un corazón sin luz. Carencia
de dolor que produce dolor: sólo la piedra,
dentro,
va creciendo. Somos lo que nunca
creímos llegar a ser. Esto hacen,
en nosotros, los otros. Sólo
todo aquello que no es un ser humano
no contribuye a nuestra nada.

Limitrophe Poems

I.

    The void is not a chair
facing the desert: it is the silence
of the soul. It is a heart
without light. It is seeing this hand
      —coming from a smaller hand,
    lost and soft perhaps—
still, but not dead: being what dies,
ashes of what was. Changing. Moving
in its profound immobility
      —thus moves . . . time.
Making itself visible on the table.
Alive, yet other. A freed object
that was a hand and now is another hand
and leaves no trace in the stone
but in sand: the water
of that great desert.
             Or a hand
that is an empty chair facing the same desert
      —I'll know what I'm saying now
    in a few years.
      A hand
that hangs from an arm that belongs to a shoulder
and this shoulder to a heart without light. Absence
of pain that produces pain: only the stone,
inside,
is growing. We are what we never
thought we'd be. This is done,
in us, by others. Only
that which is not human
does not contribute to our nothingness.

II.

    A veces no entro a tiempo en las horas
ni con buen pie,
y algo de mí se tambalea,
desentonado,
más acá o más allá
de lo real lejano.
                      Porque me quedo lejos,
vengo de lejos—sin saberlo—.
                            Lo que ata
mi atención a otro lado
no es lo que podría llamarse una memoria.
Más se parece a una raíz:
a la raíz de una memoria encadenada,
con musgo,
tras una puerta sin pestillo,
ni aldaba, ni umbrosa cerradura;
una raíz que impide
lo que de mí se espera en una hora;
una raíz a la que nunca deberé preguntar
sino saltarla
porque el tejido de sus sendas tiene enigmas profundos,
y el tiempo que sujeta mi muñeca
es testimonio
de un compromiso breve, pero cierto.

II.

    Sometimes I don't enter the hours on time
or in step,
and something in me staggers,
out of tune,
outside the limits
of the farthest reality.
                        Because I remain far,
I come from far—without knowing it.
                              What ties
my attention to another place
isn't what I'd call memory.
It's more like a root:
the root of a chained memory,
moss-filled,
behind a door without a latch,
or knocker, or a dark lock;
a root that blocks
what is expected of me at any hour;
a root that I should never question,
simply jump over
because the weave of its veins poses deep enigmas,
and time is grasping my wrist
as testimony
of brief but certain obligation.

Los dioses difíciles

I.

Vienen del agua, como náufragos que regresaran,
los años que se dejan olvidados sobre las mesas,
en maletas de ropa de veranos que, luego,
estrecha o corta,
ya no se viste nunca más y muere
bajo el definitivo olvido de una llave; en cajones,
o tras los muebles más abuelos que nunca se cambiaron de
                                                                            lugar.
                    Porque parece
que desde el mar vinieran:
húmedos hombros, empapados
los contornos y tenues de pálido verdor, gotas
cayendo de los ojos ocultos y valvados. No los abran.
                    Mejor que no los abran.
                    No, no resbalar hacia los ojos
de esos dioses que emergen,
aspirados por una luz, y que brotan,
izados, puros y podridos
—siempre presentes
y más crecidos cuanto más relegados—,
del clamor silencioso que fue su cuna y tumba.

The Grounding of Gods

I.

  They come from water, like the shipwrecked returning,
the years left behind on tables,
in suitcases filled with summer clothing
too tight or too short,
that is no longer worn and is buried
under the too solid oblivion of a key, in drawers,
or behind the oldest furniture forever in drydock.
       Because it seems
that they come from the sea:
dripping shoulders, soaked
bones and tenuous, pale green skin, drops of water
falling from the veils of valvular eyes. Don't open them.
       Better not to open them.
       No, don't slide toward the eyes
of those gods,
drawn by a light, blooming,
standing straight, pure yet corrupted
—always present,
growing even more in exile—
emerging out of the silent cry from cradle to grave.

Haldeamos por calles numerarias
ascendiendo escalera, pronunciando
no se sabe qué libros importantes.
Somos papeles muy firmados
y muchos y esenciales documentos
y más radiografías y poderes. Ayunos
de meldar en los seres que crecen sobre las aguas;
de recibir lo que transcurre entre la yerba.
           Olvidados
de que al abrirse una puerta,
al entornar los ojos como en un dormir,
o en un momento de pereza del alma,
ellos vuelven del mar donde vivían
sin que un sólo minuto les fuera indultado.
            Y al reencontrarlos,
no queremos que abran los ojos
       —aspiramos ardientemente a
            que no nos miren—,
por si llorasen por lo que ya no lloramos
        —y tenemos el firme propósito
            de ya no llorar—,
su lágrima única, rodante por la mejilla intacta
de un tiempo que el tiempo no mancilla.
   Y las horas
que se fueron puliendo y deshaciendo en arena finísima,
recobran, ante ellos, su densa y triste contextura de
              piedra.
   Y comprendemos
que en el dolor vivíamos; que esa terrible paz era
             campana
en la que un aire puro estaba destrozando
lo que es y debe ser perecedero.

We run, skirts billowing, through numbered streets,
ascending stairs, pronouncing
lord knows what important titles of books.
We are the well-signed papers,
all those essential documents
and more and more x-rays and powers to the nth.
        [The fastings
of speech in beings who rise above the waters;
are deprived of what is happening in the grass.
         We forget
that if you open a door,
half-close your eyes as in sleep,
in an idle moment of the soul,
they come back from the sea where they were living
not a single minute forgiven.
        And finding them again,
we don't want their eyes to open
    —we pray fervently
       they don't look at us—
in case they should weep when we no longer weep
    —and we are firm
       in not weeping—
a single tear, sliding down the intact cheek
of a time unstained by time.
  And, in their presence, the hours,
polished and pulverized into very fine sand,
recover the dense, sad texture of stone.
  And we see
that we were living in pain; and that terrible peace was
            a bell
in which a pure air was destroying
what is, what must perish.

II.

    Cuando tenemos los ojos azules
y la leche infinita y circular sin hiel nos alimenta
—y también sin ternura—, es impasible el tiempo
desnudo de su máscara de víctima o verdugo.
                      Luego olvidamos
y la arena, asumiendo el oficio notarial, erosiona,
sella, profana: signo, testimonio de eras.
Y devienen las épocas de la necedad, los puertos
y los nidos de la locura; el lentamente
caer mientras nos empeñamos
en horadar la piedra de los vientres maternos
con una pluma de ave de cien ojos. Las aguas
tórnanse oscuras, quietas. Calla el mundo.
                    Las ciudades
suenan lejanas y un sol bajo, de calor suave,
ilumina los lejanos hogares de la niñez, el cuarto
del primer nacimiento, la cama donde nadie
ya volverá a morir, los retratos perdidos,
los grupos familiares, las esfumadas voces . . . :
el oloroso establo de razas clausuradas.

II.

    When our eyes are still blue
and milk, infinite and round, feeds us
—plainly, simply— time stands impassive,
stripped of its mask of victim/executioner.
                   Then we forget
and sand, assuming the notary position, erodes,
seals, profanes: as a sign, witness to an era.
Then come the ages of stupidity, the ports
and nests of madness; the slow
falling down while we insist
on boring through the maternal stone of the womb
using a bird's feather with one-hundred eyes. The waters
turn dark, quiet. The world is silent.
                        Cities
sound far off and a low sun, of soft warmth,
lights up the distant hearth of childhood, the birthing room
of the first-born, the bed where no one
will ever die again, the lost portraits,
the family reunions, the vanished voices . . . :
the scented stable of a closed-in race.

    Mientras estas edades se suceden
el olvido no importa. Ni caer de uno mismo.
Más tarde la ascensión es necesaria
para no ser aniquilados;
para que nuestro incidente universal
no devenga en naufragio y resbalemos
                    —a pesar de los dioses—
hacia la leche azul
                    —que el tiempo ha agriado—,
hacia la mordedura de las viejas y despóticas madres
                    —tornada en garra su caricia
                                        antigua—
destruidas;
para que nuestro retrato no sea el de un viejo borracho
                                        cagado
al que el joven no imita y apedrean los niños;
para que alguien sin piedad no nos contemple
doblar con paso no marcial la esquina no empedrada.
                    No insistir
en lo que nunca llega: abandonar el sueño de los
                                        príncipes,
la voz que oímos en la copa umbría y que no suena;
                                        los espejos
del más allá y los anillos ofrecidos.
La espera será breve. Una ola
nos llevará en su cresta transparente.
Una ola interior. No hay otra alguna.

While these ages come to pass
forgetting doesn't matter. Nor falling away from oneself.
Later the climb up becomes necessary
to avoid annihilation;
so our universal passage
won't go under and slide
        —despite the gods—
toward the blue bed
        —that time has made bitter—
toward the bite of old, despotic mothers
        —their early caresses turned
                to claws—
destroyed;
so we won't be the snapshot of a shitty old
                drunk
young men shun and children stone;
so someone pitiless won't look at us
turning the unpaved corner with an unmartial step.
    Don't insist
on the never arriving: forget about the dreams
                of princes,
the voice we hear in the shady bower, that makes no
sound;
                the mirrors
from beyond and the offered rings.
The wait will be brief. A wave
will take us in a clear crest.
An inner wave. There isn't any other.

Tregua

    Las horas de vigilia se fueron anunciando,
como un leve y lejano punto de luz,
entre un dormir y un despertar.
Luz que, en el horizonte, se fue elevando, altísima,
solitaria en la playa del final de la tierra
e invadió, lentamente, todos los territorios.
                                 Ahora
sólo espero el silencio de ese inmenso día
que a todos los abarca. En esta orilla,
por esa claridad maternal y templada
que los guardó, regresan
los que creía pasto del olvido
        —tiempo, padre, cuentas mi propia historia
          para cerrar mis ojos con piedad y despacio—:
veo alzarse las manos que me fueron propias,
mirar que poseí, cabello
que me fueron cortando, sobre el suelo
        —qué brillo, qué esplendor,
          cuánta esperanza bajo la tijera—.
                                Regresan
como cuerpos que olas devolvieran
        —náufragos y salvados,
          ardientes y distantes—,
                                con la misma
inquietud que los días no borraron,
con la misma pequeña desventura
interior, y el desamparo
que tan propio les fuera, sobre el hombro.
        —Cuántos años mirándote a la cara, mundo,
          para saber si te gustaba
          mi manera de atarme los zapatos—.
Aquí, bajo esto a lo que llamo luz,
he recogido suficientes violetas
para ponerlas, mundo, sobre tu aprobación
        —que ya no espero—;
sobre tu olvido
        —que ya he dejado de temer—.

Truce

    The hours of the watch went on being announced,
like a far-away, fragile point of light,
between sleeping and waking.
A light that went on rising, high in the horizon,
solitary on the sands of earth's end
and slowly invaded every territory.
                                        Now
I'm only waiting for the silence of that vast day
that will sweep in everybody. On this shore,
guarded in maternal,
tempered brightness, they are returning,
those I thought lay in fields of oblivion
       —time enough, father, to tell my own story
         to close my eyes slowly in pity—
I see hands rise that once were mine,
look at what I possessed, hair
they went on cutting, on the floor
       —how it shone and sparkled,
         how much hope lies under the scissors.
                                They are returning
like bodies that the waves give back
       —shipwrecked and salvaged,
       passionate and distant—
                                 with the same
anxiety that wouldn't go away,
with the same small, inner
misery, and the being marooned
so very much theirs, on their shoulders.
       —How many years have I been looking in your
                                    [face, world,
    just to know if you liked
    the way I tied my shoes.
Here, under what I call a kind of light,
I've gathered enough violets, world,
to blanket your approval
       —I don't expect it anymore—
and your amnesia
       —I don't fear it anymore.

From: *Del camino de humo*

Busco señales en la piedra ...

Busco señales en la piedra
que ordena sombra y luz, cuadra
el círculo y lo sostiene
sobre el yacente corazón y, alta abuela del mundo,
almohadilla relatos en su agostada piel.
Busco signos que ya no animan
lo que contaron pero laten
con helado fulgor que nos excede
y derrumba. Busco
lo que quiere ser dicho de nuevo y espera, y
debe ser resucitado
a pesar del musgo y el viento,
de la lluvia, del hierro de los hombres
y su tesón para demoler; del reinado
de la basura
y las dolencias de los seres sin vida.
Dedos que llaman desde la piedra,
garzas que murmuran, batallas
inmóviles, caracoles
sobre el acanto sin espinas, detenido
su milenario caminar.
                Ultimas luces,
derramadas por el ocaso,
mojan el bulto de unos montes, lejos.

From: *Road of Smoke*

I Look for Signs in the Stone

I look for signs in the stone,
a setting for shadow and light,
a square of the circle, sustaining it
over the sleeping heart and, like the great grandmother
                              [of the world,
sheltering stories in her burned-out skin.
I look for signs that no longer sing
their stories, but beat with frozen fire,
overflowing and caving us in. I look
for what wants to be said again,
waits, and needs to be revived
in spite of the moss and the wind,
in spite of the rain, the iron of men,
the stiff ravaging thrust
in spite of the reign of rubbish
and the aches of lifeless beings.
Fingers calling from stone,
whispering herons, paralyzed
battles, snails atop the thornless acanthus,
millennial crawl stopped.
                Last lights,
spilling into sunset,
soak the shapes of far-off mountains.

            (¿De allí vinieron?).
            Y la piedra
se adormece de nuevo con un suspiro.
                    Desciende
la noche; libera
sus criaturas de silencio y sombra,
y disuelve los lugares de tránsito en espera
de otro día, otros pasos.

                    Y no tengo luz
                    aunque venga de ella.

                    Signos
que nos miran llegar y desaparecer
con la esperanza de ser llenados de nuevo,
calentados con la saliva de nuestra edad,
repetidos, multiplicados
en un rumor de hombres y martillos.
                            Manos
que se tienden, bocas sin voz.
                    Y otra noche
borrándolos.

                (Did they come from there?)
                And the stone
falls asleep again with a sigh.
                Night
descends, frees its creatures of silence and shadow,
dissolves sites of passage in hopes
of another day, other footsteps.

                        Coming from the light,
                        I have no light.

                        Signs
that see us arrive and disappear,
hoping to be filled once more,
warmed with spit,
repeated, multiplied in our time,
in a murmur of men and mallets.
                        Hands
outstretched, voiceless mouths.
                        And another night
rubbing them out.

Profundo como los ríos

> *"My soul has grown deep like the rivers."*
> Langston Hughes

Rostro negro de soledad,
en tu sudor toco la nieve que se abrió en el aire.
Regresan las agujas de hielo bajo el sol,
y me encuentro, al perderme, en el lino cuajado
o en el deshielo súbito
de otra mañana:
aquella en que el narciso despertaba
a su esplendor efímero.
Amado rostro negro de soledad, tocarte desearía;
recoger en mi uña el destello de ese sudor
como si recogiera, uno a uno, los días que te envolvieron
y hablaba como tú.
Y, sobre todo, me rebelaba con esperanza.
                Tu casa está sobre el jaspe y el zafiro,
                sobre la calcedonia y la esmeralda,
                y sobre las otras siete fundamentales
                sin exceptuar la amatista.
                Los vientos, por ti, se han detenido en
                          sus cuatro lugares.
                        De soledad
        están pobladas tus calles. Y de lejanía
        oculta tras doseles de arena.

Deep Like Rivers

"My soul has grown deep like the rivers."
Langston Hughes

Black face of solitude,
with your sweat I touch snow opened into air,
needles of ice under the sun return,
and I find myself, by losing myself, in thickened flax
or in sudden thaw
of another morning:
when narcissus unfolding
woke to swift splendor.
Beloved face black with solitude, let me touch you;
let me glean with my fingernail the shine of that sweat
as if gleaning, one by one, all your days,
as if I spoke like you.
Most of all, as if I could resist with hope.
        Your house is built on jasper and sapphire;
        chalcedony and emerald,
        and the seven precious stones
        including the amethyst.
        The winds, for you, have stopped
                in their four points.
            Your streets
        are peopled with solitude. And with hidden
        distance behind canopies of sand.

En las noches de estruendo y orgía,
copas volcadas y cruces llameantes,
has ocultado tu corazón bajo una gardenia
y la armonía, desde tus manos,
	—Si yo volviera, ¿adónde volvería?—
ha embriagado las sombras.
	Si yo volviera,
dibujaría en la pared de mi prisión
nombres fugaces, las palabras
de una antigua canción, un teléfono viejo
con el cable cortado sobre el pecho
de una mañana, un libro sin abrir,
el blanco sobre el verde
y un ave del Camino de las Ocas.
También lo que traías, rostro negro de soledad.

On nights of revel and riot,
of broken glasses and flaming crosses,
you hid your heart under a gardenia
and raptured shadows
with the harmony of hands.
      —If I came back, where would I go?—
      If I came back,
I would draw on the wall of my prison
fugitive names, the words
of an old song, an old telephone number
with the cable cut over the breast
of a morning, an unopened book,
white over green
a bird from the flight of wild geese.
And what you brought, black face of solitude.

Orden del sueño

II.

Cerré los ojos a la luz sin nombre
y los abrí en el sitio
del que nunca me fui aunque los días pasen
y las formas—las sombras—, los sonidos
la turbamulta del color, los arduos
desvelos se alíen y sacudan
                sus iracundos puños ante mí.
                Nunca me fui
porque quedó pendiente una respuesta;
porque quedó escindida una palabra;
porque quedaron trozos en el suelo
clamando por imagen, por sentido,
por unidad que sólo el sueño otorga
        —quebrado el vaso,
          perdida el agua—,
e impone, al despertar, una paz llena
de vivida ocasión, de encuentro cierto.
   La amistad entre sombras
reúne cuerpos muy distantes,
devuelve, sin ruptura, las voces ya olvidadas
y pone en las palabras—su reflejo—
                la razón nunca oída.
                       De esos seres
yo no tengo recuerdo
            —son quienes nunca fuimos—
            pero sé que son ciertos,
y su callado paso, bajo la luz sin sombras,
deja huella en el mundo que toco y que no es firme
aunque en él caiga, sola, cuando los ojos abro.

The Order of Dream*

II.

I closed my eyes to the nameless light
and I opened them in the place
I never left, though days pass
and forms—shadows— sounds,
the rabble of color, hard
sleepless nights band together and shake
                              angry fists at me.
                              I never left
because an answer was pending;
because a word was severed;
because they ended up in pieces on the floor
screaming for an image, a sense,
a unity that only dream confers
                          —the glass broken,
                            the water lost—
only dream imposes, in waking, a peace
full of lived time, of certain encounter.
    Friendship among shadows
reunites separated bodies,
returns, seamless, voices already forgotten
and places in words—in its reflection—
                            forever unheard reason.
                            Of those beings
I have no memory
                  —we were never them—
                  but I know they exist,
and their muted step, under shadowless light,
leaves a trace in the world that I touch, that is not solid,
even though I fall into it, alone, when I open my eyes.

---

*The first part of this poem appeared in *Ancient Secret Voices of the Night* (see p.182). It has turned into the first of four poems, written at different times and moods, but which taken together now occupy their corresponding place in her work.

III.

En el principio sólo fue una espalda,
una obstinada nuca, oscuro
el cabello que ya no puede ser.

> (Veló la luna de los sueños
> a quien mostrarse no quería).

Pero la lluvia, los ponientes,
el musgo, el llanto que supuran
los zapatos, la ropa, las columnas
que se rompen, se aja, se desploman;
la sombra que nos deja en un camino,
y la candela, o la ceniza,
fuego de ayer, esplendor del vacío

> —nada muda, si el tiempo no la hiere,
> la persistente voluntad de un sueño—,

al rostro oculto condujeron
hasta la luz.
    En el silencio
    —y en sombra interna—,
el rostro, preservado de la ofensa del tiempo,
era aún el que fue un día ya olvidado.

IV.

El despertar me dijo un día
que acaso un sueño es eco de otro sueño.

III.

In the beginning it was only a shoulder,
an obstinate nape of the neck,
dark hair, impossible now.

        (The moon of dreams kept watch over a body,
        but refused to show herself.)

While the rain and the setting suns,
the moss, the tears leaking
from shoes, clothing, columns
that break, wrinkle, crumble;
the shadow that leaves us alone in the road,
and the candle, or the ash,
yesterday's fire, the splendor of the void

        —nothing changes, if time does not wound it,
        the persistent will of a dream—

led the hidden face
toward the light.
        In the silence
        —and inward shadow—
the face, preserved from time's offense,
was still what it was on a day long forgotten.

IV.

It was waking up told me one day
that maybe a dream is the echo of another dream.

CODA

Vitrina

> *Para Eduardo y María del Carmen,*
> *que conocieron a las últimas.*

Las niñas ya se han ido
cada una a su propia anciana,
zagalejos de espuma
botitas de caña.

Las niñas ya se han muerto
—cada una fue su propia anciana—
y en la alacena dejaron
las lunas blancas.

Se olvidaron las niñas
de todas sus palabras
y de todos los príncipes
con que valsaban.

Se dejaron las niñas
agujas ensartadas
y en aquellos estrados
por donde pasaban

las luces encendidas,
las tazas, empezadas,
y el aire menudito
que las espabilaba.

CODA

Dollhouse

*For Eduardo and María del Carmen,
who knew the last of them.*

They're gone now, the dear girls,
slipped inside an old maid,
floating in petticoats of foam
and sweet cane of boots inlaid.

They're dead now, the dear girls,
—turned old and white—
storing in the cupboard
pale moondrops of light,

having lost, the dear girls,
their words of wit
the shining princes
the waltz they lit.

The needles are threaded
and left behind, like lasses
who wait in drawing rooms
and one by one each passes.

The lights are blazing,
the teacups sipped,
and as the air is music,
so like spirits gaily they tripped.

Las niñas que se fueron
se llevaron las llaves de sus casas
y parece que vienen por otras galerías
a recoger las cosas olvidadas.

Y no hay quien las espere
porque son otras manos más lejanas
las que alisaban sus encajes
y trenzaban sus trenzas apagadas.

Si sus voces se oyeran por los sueños
ya no hay quien sepa a qué sonaban;
si algún rostro aparece en otro rostro
ya no los reconoce la mirada.

Por calles sin memoria,
cuadernos amarillos y sábanas de holanda,
las que iban a ser ya fueron y pasaron
enhebrando sus sombras a sombras que llegaban.

They went away, the dear girls,
the keys to home in their hands,
wandering through other passageways
and gathering things forgot in bands.

But no one waits for them
and other hands smoothed their lacy dresses,
and distant hands
wound their faded tresses.

If their voices could be heard in dreams
no one now would know the sound;
and if a face appears in another face
the look on their faces would not be found.

Through streets with no memory,
a yellowed notebook and linen sheet,
those to be were no more and pass,
threading their shadows to the shadows they meet.

Recuerdo de una calle

Si súbitamente volviese a estar en ti,
sobre tu herido asfalto,
no tendrías quizá tus límites borrosos
entre nieves y grises salpicados de sol,
ni tu apariencia de camino hacia dentro.
Te recuerdo desierta,
imaginada: no sé ni dónde
tu nombre estaba escrito.
Pero así, tú y yo, somos reales:
se es más real no siendo
sino memoria. Jugo del tiempo,
restos de un fuego efímero
en el que nada ya nos puede acontecer.

En esa calle no había muertos
ni por morir. Los vacíos
aún no se habían diseñado,
tampoco los espacios perdidos
pesaban como ahora, mas eras tan pretérita,
tan de camino estabas a tu imagen de ahora,
que me veo sentada en la butaca
—que entonces no veía: la madera
muy clara de la mesa brilla bajo la luz. Fuera,
los monjes del invierno—y cierro un libro
que nunca acabaría de leer.
      Este regalo
de tiempo unas palabras
lo pusieron de nuevo en la calle de ahora,
en la mesa de ahora y en sus libros
que, con frecuencia, tan sólo leo a medias.
Como allí.

Memory of a Street

If, suddenly, I were in you once again,
on your wounded asphalt,
maybe your edges wouldn't be so blurred,
somewhere between snowwhites and grays spattered
                                          [with sun,
or your appearance like a road turned inward.
I remember you deserted,
imaginary: I don't even know where
your name was written down.
But just the same you and I, we're real:
Memory makes us more real. Drops of time,
debris of fleeting fire
where nothing can touch us anymore.

There were no dead or dying
on that street. Vacant lots
hadn't yet been designed,
and lost spaces weren't millstones
like now, but you were so much the past,
so working toward your present image,
that I see myself again, sitting in the armchair
—which I couldn't see then: the pale wood
of the desk is shining beneath the light. Outside,
are the monks of winter—then I close a book
that I'd never finish.
                    This gift
of time a few words
was replayed on the street I live in now,
on the desk I have now and in the books
I usually only get halfway through.
Like before.